FILM STARS

Stars are an integral part of every major film industry in the world.
In this pivotal new series, each book is devoted to an international
movie star, looking at the development of their identity, their acting
and performance methods, the cultural significance of their work,
and their influence and legacy. Taking a wide range of different stars,
including George Clooney, Brigitte Bardot and Dirk Bogarde
among others, this series encompasses the sphere of silent and sound
acting, Hollywood and non-Hollywood areas of cinema, and child and
adult forms of stardom. With its broad range, but a focus throughout
on the national and historical dimensions to film, the series offers
students and researchers a new approach to studying film.

SERIES EDITORS
Martin Shingler and Susan Smith

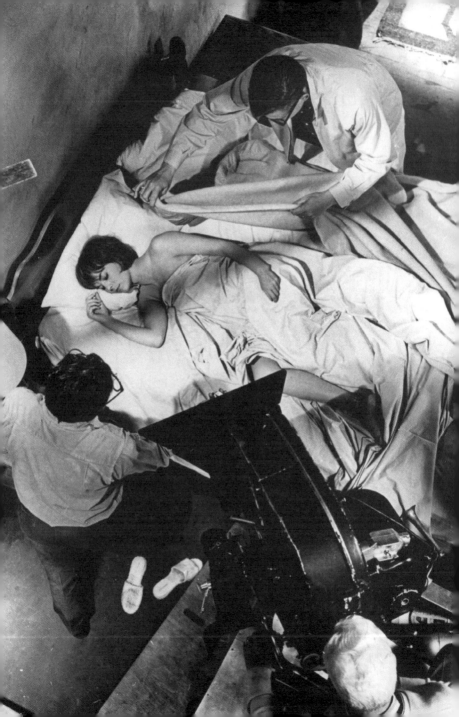

Natalie WOOD

REBECCA SULLIVAN

ALWAYS BE A STAR!

Rebecca Sullivan

Feb '18

palgrave

A BFI book published by Palgrave

First published in 2016 by
PALGRAVE

on behalf of the

BRITISH FILM INSTITUTE
21 Stephen Street, London W1T 1LN
www.bfi.org.uk

There's more to discover about film and television through the BFI. Our world-renowned archive, cinemas, festivals, films, publications and learning resources are here to inspire you.

PALGRAVE in the UK is an imprint of Macmillan Publishers Limited, registered in England, company number 785998, of 4 Crinan Street, London N1 9XW. Palgrave Macmillan in the US is a division of St Martin's Press LLC, 175 Fifth Avenue, New York, NY 10010. Palgrave is a global imprint of the above companies and is represented throughout the world. Palgrave® and Macmillan® are registered trademarks in the United States, the United Kingdom, Europe and other countries.

Designed by couch
Cover images: (front) *West Side Story* (Robert Wise and Jerome Robbins, 1961), © Beta Productions (courtesy of United Artists/Photofest); (back) Natalie Wood, 1964 (courtesy of Photofest)

Set by Cambrian Typesetters, Camberley, Surrey
Printed in China

This book is printed on paper suitable for recycling and made from fully managed and sustained forest sources. Logging, pulping and manufacturing processes are expected to conform to the environmental regulations of the country of origin.

British Library Cataloguing-in-Publication Data
A catalogue record for this book is available from the British Library
A catalog record for this book is available from the Library of Congress

ISBN 978–1–84457–637–1

(*previous page*) On the set of *Inside Daisy Clover* (1965)

CONTENTS

ACKNOWLEDGMENTS

My gratitude first is for the series editors, Martin Shingler and Susan Smith, who received my proposal enthusiastically and provided insightful guidance throughout every stage. Jenna Steventon, Lucinda Knight, Chantal Latchford and Sophia Contento at Palgrave have been generous and patient with me. Incisive critiques and much-needed support along the way came from Tamar Jeffers McDonald, Kirsten Pullen and Cynthia Lucia. I especially want to thank Keir Keightley, who would talk Natalie with me for hours. I was fortunate to teach a course on Natalie Wood in the University of Calgary Film Studies programme. Nothing helps provide clarity for complex ideas quite like teaching them, and so I must credit my students with many of the arguments in this book.

When I first mentioned to my sister, Louise, that I was thinking about writing a book on Natalie Wood, she replied, 'Well yes, you've always loved her.' Even I hadn't realised that all my favourite films starred her until that moment. So, to her I say thank you for that and so much more.

My husband, Bart Beaty, and son, Sebastian Beaty, are always by my side and give me so much strength and happiness. To my mother, who watched old movies with me, and to my father, who watches them with me still.

INTRODUCTION

In 1961, although she was at the height of her fame, Natalie Wood was dismissed by *Newsweek* as the least remarkable actress of the era:

Kim Novak is perpetually surrounded by the color lavender; Elizabeth Taylor is fragile and intense; Marilyn Monroe is as natural as all indoors. – and all of them are insecurely searching for the meaning of life. Thanks to personality and press agentry, these images are indelibly stamped on the public mind. But the image machine has been remarkably remiss with Natalie Wood, who, to the public at large, conjures up the biggest blank of any major actress in Hollywood. ('Tragedy in Overdrive' 1961, 102).

Twenty years later, in one of the last profiles before her tragic death by drowning, another magazine was able, with the benefit of hindsight, to define her significance to American film. She was, quite simply, 'our sexual conscience on the silver screen' ('Natalie Wood' 1980, 118). In both her acting and her public star profile, Wood performed a host of contradictory and conflicting roles that imbricated mid-twentieth-century anxieties about gender, sexuality, race and class into a portrait of modern American womanhood in transition (Lucia 2012, 54). Wood reached the pinnacle of her career at a particularly volatile moment in Hollywood history, as the studio system collapsed and audiences clamoured for heightened levels of authenticity and social relevance from their cinematic entertainment.

At the same time, there was also a longing for imagined simpler days where everyone knew their place and social conflicts could be resolved with a few psychological tricks. With no set conviction about what the next generation of women should be like, Wood's elusive persona was entirely in step with the times.

Wood did not merely play the role of the woman uncertain about what she wants on screen, but also in her public role as star. As one fan magazine put it, 'Natalie Wood's life imitates art – the sad, lost, searching, lonely role she plays on the screen' (Hoffman 1962, 88). In her childhood, she was the precocious and wise-beyond-her-years daughter of Russian immigrants who was leading her family to the American Dream. By her teens, she was dubbed a 'junior femme fatale' for her wild antics and swinging dating life. Married at nineteen to matinee idol Robert Wagner (eight years her senior), she refashioned herself as part of Hollywood's golden couple. After the collapse of their marriage in 1962, and at the peak of her stardom, she wavered uncertainly between the glamour of Old Hollywood and the introspection of an emergent New American Cinema that was characterised by New York-trained Method actors and directors. Ultimately, she sided with stardom in part to shield herself from too much psychological exposure on screen (Moore 1984b, 52; Pecheco 1979, 36). By the mid-sixties, she was the favourite whipping post of critics who called her 'a perfect little Eloise doll' (Wolfe 1968, 283), and 'the most machine-tooled of Hollywood ingénues' (Kael 1962, 35). So from 1966 until 1969, she turned her back on Hollywood, speaking to the media only occasionally to discuss her daily psychoanalysis, her art collecting or her studies at UCLA (Bart 1966; Lewis 1968; Whitman 1967). At the time of her comeback at thirty, she was a confident, experienced actor, who was also every inch a Hollywood star. Through the seventies, after a re-marriage to Wagner and the birth of her two daughters, she exuded a level of contentment that seemed out of step with the neuroses of the Me Decade (Wolfe 1976). As a

Splendor in the Grass (1961) (BFI)

Hollywood maven, she was a stalwart defender of old-style glamour and sophistication, of liberal family values and of her rightful place in the pantheon of stardom. And then, in 1981, as she was once again wavering between the roles of star and actor, devoted housewife and sexual libertine, Wood stumbled into the stormy waters off Catalina Island and drowned.

As an actress, Wood teetered precariously on the edge of greatness in some of her films, frustrating those who believed in her talent. Elia Kazan, her director in *Splendor in the Grass* (1961) defended her vigorously in the press. 'You say she's been good in *only* two pictures? Then, I say she's got it. Two pictures is a hell of a lot of pictures' (Zimmerann 1963, 92). The two pictures to which he was referring were, of course, his own, and that of his directing protégé,

Nicholas Ray, who made *Rebel Without a Cause* (1955). Both are considered classics of mid-century Method style, but Wood was in every way a daughter of Hollywood. As she sought to develop her acting skills, she drew liberally from both studio-style star acting and Method in ways that, while not always successful, encompassed the complexity and confusion befuddling the country. Although Wood ultimately sided with star acting principles, it was Method directors who drew out her best performances. She remained intrigued by Method acting throughout her career but decided that she worked better at a psychological distance.

To me, the only way you can be honest is to relate something to yourself and do it the way you feel it inside you. If you don't believe it yourself, you can't do it honestly. I think acting has to be on instinct – you have to use 'the method' without realizing it (Gehman 1957b, 92).

While Wood always spoke appreciatively about Ray and Kazan, she also readily admitted that working under the Method system caused a lot of damage to her already fragile psyche. '"It was a rough period for me", Nat says, taking a guilty puff from her cigarette and recalling those times when her personal life appeared to intersect with her more neurotic film roles' (Pecheco 1979, 36). The psychological toll forced her to forego roles that may have cemented her status as a great actress. She could have starred with her ex-lover Warren Beatty in the New American Cinema masterpiece *Bonnie and Clyde* (1967). Instead, she starred in the mercifully forgettable sex romp *Penelope* (1966), a film so bad that it convinced her to take a three-year hiatus from film-making. Her ambivalence about her acting style and career decisions became a hallmark of her stardom. As one magazine said of her, 'The beautiful star confuses and is confused by the three roles she must play: the actress on the screen, the public personality the press agents create for her and the person she really is' (Lyle 1961, 83).

Kirsten Pullen provides a succinct overview of how Hollywood acting styles in the decades following World War II underwent a massive transformation in line with growing social anxieties over self and society, authenticity and social responsibility (2014, 9). Naturalism remained the dominant paradigm, demanding a unified relationship between actor and role so that emotions appeared genuine and motivations believable. Studio-based naturalism focused mostly on exposés of stars' romantic relationships, private homes and social lives to shore up their star identity. James Naremore defines studio acting as a combination of role, actor and image that is simultaneously spectacular and comfortably familiar (1988, 15). By contrast, Method demanded a psychological evaluation of the role through introspection and self-revelation (Butler 1991, 9). Thus, as Method acting gained a foothold in Hollywood during the 1950s, actors were increasingly required to offer glimpses into their creative process as an extension of their psychological selves. Cynthia Baron and Sharon Marie Carnicke mark this dramatic shift in Hollywood acting styles with a 1957 *Life* magazine article that featured none other than Natalie Wood (2008, 25). While the most intense of the Method actors – such as James Dean, Wood's co-star in *Rebel Without a Cause* – refused any intrusion into their private lives, Wood consistently traversed the precarious boundary line between the two competing systems of naturalist acting. By being neither one nor the other, Wood became something altogether unique, 'an unambiguous marker of change' (Lucia 2012, 26).

Key to Wood's contradictory image was her preternatural physicality. She was extremely petite, but had hauntingly big, dark, brown eyes that overwhelmed her otherwise tiny features. Frequently Wood was described as some elusive mix of child and woman – the exact measurements of which slowly reversed themselves as she matured. She was not a tempestuous sexpot, rather her 'dark, fresh loveliness' was only 'slightly sensuous' ('Born to Be a Star' 1963, 182).

Natalie Wood portraits by Margaret Keane
(1961) (Photofest)

'She is not [a sex figure],' another profile of the time insisted, 'What
sets her apart, both on the screen and personally, more than
anything else is the avidity of her small, waif-like face with its large,
hyper-attentive eyes' (Maynard 1964, X7). That physically uncanny
presence not only elucidated anxieties over women's sexual maturity
but also hinted at the racial and ethnic conflicts dividing the
country. Wood was born in America to Russian immigrant parents
and never tried to hide that heritage. Her dark colouring made her
believable enough within Hollywood's racist casting practices of the
time to play roles in which her racial identity compromised her
sexual purity. Creating even more confusion were those roles where

her working-class status was signified through associations with racial minority culture, a common trope in mid-century American popular culture (Breines 2001; Dyer 1997; Medovoi 2005). More often than not, that disorderly triangulation of sexual-racial-class identities in her films resulted in her descent into hysterical madness resolved either by grim capitulation to a life without passion or, occasionally, death. In a Freudian-infused era, where women's sexuality was unproblematically considered 'a dark continent' (Arbiser 2013), the sexually ambivalent woman, veering recklessly between the poles of white respectability and dark desire, represented the volatility of the age and held serious implications for sexual, racial and class politics.

Perhaps it is because of that ambiguous, transitional role that, even in her heyday, film critics could claim that she was not much more than a 'blank'. Moreover, mention Wood today and few recognise the name immediately unless films like *Rebel Without a Cause* or *West Side Story* (1961) are mentioned. Tragically, Wood is less remembered for her films than she is for her mysterious death. Conspiracy theories that she did not slip off the boat in a drunken haze but was thrown off in a moment of fury by her jealous husband cannot be addressed here. What is more important is how the story of her death fits neatly into a lifelong narrative of a woman who never quite knew what she wanted and was tormented by perpetual yearning for whatever it was that she didn't have. At the time of her death, Wood was working with Christopher Walken, part of the inner circle of New American Cinema that had taken Method acting to dizzying heights. At home looking after their children was Robert Wagner, who wished Wood would remain in Los Angeles and maybe seek out steady television roles like he had done, putting her domestic duties first. During a cruise on their yacht *The Splendour* (named after her most famous movie which had also caused their first marriage to end), Wagner and Walken fought viciously over what Wood should be: actress/rebel or star/mother. Outraged, Wood stormed out of the cabin and ultimately, to her death. Without that terrible end, and all the questions that it leaves behind, it is not clear whether Wood's legacy would have lingered as long as it has. It seems the greatest poetic injustice that the actor who personified an in-between culture that could not agree on what its women should be, died as a result of that very confusion.

This book seeks to rectify Wood's legacy by recognising her enormous, albeit uneven, contributions to Hollywood both as an actor and as a star. Neglect of Wood's career says more about the film industry's treatment of women than it does about her lasting significance. Certainly, many of her films are considered classics of mid-century cinema and continue to be screened and discussed at length. Yet, that occurs without acknowledging that she is the linchpin connecting such otherwise disparate films as *Rebel Without a Cause*, *West Side Story*, *Inside Daisy Clover* (1965) and *Bob & Carol & Ted & Alice* (1969). It begs the question: what more can we learn about American cinema history by examining it from the position of a disregarded figure? The answer to that question begins with a reassessment of the well-worn but decidedly under-theorised character of the ingénue.

There has been surprisingly little written about the ingénue, a stock character that remains the most reliable stepping stone to cinematic stardom for young actresses. The ingénue combines a fragile innocence with sexual desirability. The allure of the desecrated virgin has been a mainstay of fiction across genres and forms for centuries, fraught with hidden longing and the uneasy suspicion that she may be a willing victim. In Wood's time, the ingénue role shifted from one where the threat to her purity was external to one where it was her own psychological frailty that could lead her astray. In other words, no man could save her unless she herself was willing to be saved. Yet, even as the American sexual revolution kicked into high gear, Hollywood grew uncomfortable with the sexually savvy ingénue. With the advent of New American Cinema, representations of women's sexual autonomy became secondary and supportive to men's sexual-neurotic psyches (Mordden 1990, 77; Wexman 1993, 168). Studying Wood's career through the lens of the ingénue provides insight not only into this central but under-theorised character, but also into American cinema's ongoing confused and contradictory sexual scripts for women.

Chapter 1 explores Wood's apprenticeship in the studio acting system through the films *Tomorrow Is Forever* (1946) and *Miracle on 34th Street* (1947). It also reflects on the close connections between film and social policy at the time by studying the nearly forgotten propaganda film, *The Green Promise* (1949). The chapter reflects on the development of Wood's acting style by identifying many of the characteristic tropes that she relied upon throughout her career: a cocked head, raised eyebrows, widening eyes, precocious giggles, taut body and overflowing tears. It also examines the immense pressure placed on her to not only be a good actor, but to be a good worker: to do what she was told no matter what, to never question the director or studio executives, to treat stardom as a duty and a calling. Her compliancy amazed many of her directors and co-stars who often praised her as wise beyond her years. Interestingly, as she matured, the press was more likely to call her out for bratty behaviour, denigrate her intellect and regard her as nothing more than a 'boy-crazy teenager' ('Boy-crazy' 1956, 34).

Chapter 2 explores Wood's two greatest teenage roles and argues that together, they offer a picture of a young woman teetering on the brink of too much sexual independence. *Rebel Without a Cause* and *Splendor in the Grass* present Wood as the sexual hysteric in the social-problem picture. They showcase Wood's ability to surpass herself when working with strong-willed, paternalistic directors. As one magazine claimed:

Some actresses are vessels for a director, and what he pours into them must sink. In many roles, Natalie Wood came out cloudy. Her friends put this down to addled direction. One says, 'Natalie needs an enlightened director. Look, it's easier to find the atom bomb's secrets if you have Einstein helping you instead of the corner grocer' (Zimmerann 1963, 92).

It is not coincidence that her success in these roles had less to do with her Hollywood training and more to do with the influences of New York Method acting. The argument here is not that Wood was a Method actor – her flirtation with the Actors Studio was brief and she was as likely to ridicule it as to praise it. However, it is in the tensions between Hollywood star acting and the grittier and more psychologically complex Method acting that Wood's acting style crystallised. Critics who had given up on Wood now saw in her 'a very knowledgeable and yet thoroughly natural actress. Her style is luminous and intimate, somewhere between the assertive personality stars of old and the chameleon-like youngsters of the Actor's studio' ('Movie Star into Actress' 1962, 54).

Chapter 3 continues the exploration of Wood as sexual hysteric by investigating the racial and class ambiguity of many of her characters. Two films in particular stand out, more for their failure than their success. *Kings Go Forth* (1958) and *All the Fine Young Cannibals* (1960) are at best camp classics that even in their time were critical and box-office disappointments. They were, however, films that Wood eagerly sought out in the hope that they would secure her reputation as a serious actress. The films offer superficial commentary on civil rights by associating African Americanness with both cultural authenticity and illicit desire. Because of Wood's dark features, she was often cast in 'passing' roles, while her waifish physique downplayed any provocative sexuality that might alert the attention of censors. More important, she skilfully swung from tightly controlled to hysterical and back again, and orchestrated body, voice and eyes together into a cataclysm of competing desires against violent social forces.

While Wood continued to select roles that skirted the edges of sexual danger, she pulled back from the intensity of the Method and very publicly sided with stardom. Chapter 4 explores the last decade of her career, during which Wood basked in the glow of contented, conventional femininity, both on screen and off. After two decades of conflicting direction and debilitating demands on her physical and emotional limits, Wood now insisted on an acting style that drew on her real-life experiences and more assured sense of self. She defended the star-acting system in which she was steeped, but defined it in a more instinctual, psychologically inflected manner clearly influenced by the Method. This chapter focuses on her first comeback film after a three-year hiatus in the mid-sixties, *Bob & Carol & Ted & Alice* and her final completed film, *The Last Married Couple in America* (1980) as rare Hollywood studies of women in middle age looking back with satisfaction, not regret, at their sexual journey.

Chronicling a career spanning nearly forty years and encompassing a life from age five till her death at forty-three means that there will be obvious gaps and oversights. Some cinematic favourites, like *Marjorie Morningstar* (1958) (Sullivan 2010), *Gypsy* (1962) and *Love with the Proper Stranger* (1963) (Leibman 1992) are missing from this book. Their absence only points to the possibility of more scholarly critique on Wood to deepen understanding of women's sexuality in the postwar era, and to query why Hollywood abandoned such cinematic investigations. This book encapsulates the importance of an actress who more than anyone else represented a generation of women confused by, experimenting with, and struggling over women's sexual agency and authenticity. It is within that deeply troubled space that Wood's legacy can be reappraised and fully appreciated.

1 THE CHILD-WOMAN

It is a Hollywood truism that child stars can rarely transition to adult careers and are stranded in a netherworld where a 'normal life' can never be found (O'Connor 2008, 2). Natalie Wood is just one example of a juvenile performer who resists this cultural trope and thus demands more nuanced analysis of the cinematic child. Debuting in Hollywood in 1946, she was among the last of a generation of child actors to be fully immersed in the studio system. As Dick Moore, a former child star, recalls,

> The 1930s and 1940s in America were a throwback to the Dickensian era a century earlier, when children were perceived as little adults. Important to Hollywood's economy and the public's need for escape, each of us was a representation, a cliché (1984a, ix).

By the end of World War II, however, as prosperity and stability returned to America, the escapist fantasy offered by such Depression-era darlings as Shirley Temple was tempered by more topical fare that invoked New Deal aspirations around childhood and the future of the nation. Wood featured in many such films that recast childhood as a collective project of nation-building. In the decade that encompassed her debut cameo in Irving Pichel's *Happy Land* (1943), at the age of five, through to 1952, when her career temporarily transitioned to television, Wood appeared in eighteen features, thirteen of which were filmed between 1946–50. Granted, many of the films from Wood's childhood career are forgettable, and she was never expected to carry a film as its lead star. She was most often cast as the kid sister or precocious surrogate daughter, there to provide adorableness and comic relief.

Wood's acting success as a child was based on her ability to play a 'no-frills' child, unbedecked by ribbons, ringlets or ruffles. In plain clothes and severe braids, Wood seemed almost excessively average but for one feature: her large brown eyes. Always small for her age, Wood's tiny frame barely took up any space on screen while her thin, high voice was easily drowned out by the declamatory vocal style of co-stars like Orson Welles, Maureen O'Hara and Walter Brennan. So she learned at an early age how to use her most distinctive feature to divert attention from her adult co-stars and overwhelm the screen with emotion. In *Tomorrow Is Forever*, Wood plays an Austrian war orphan brought to America by her guardian, a physically and psychologically scarred veteran played by Welles. In her best-known feature, *Miracle on 34th Street*, she plays Susan Walker, the sceptical daughter of a bitter divorcée who, with the help of a fatherly neighbour and Santa Claus, learns how to be a child. Finally, in *The Green Promise*, an independently financed piece of propaganda for postwar agricultural policy, she plays the youngest child of a farming family, who defies her stubborn libertarian father and becomes a member of the 4-H Club, a rural youth achievement organisation operated by the Department of Agriculture.

When stars like Jackie Coogan, Shirley Temple and the Our Gang children ruled the box office, the child actor was a fantastical figure almost completely unmoored from family life, whose interactions with adults were as an equal. A child star was expected to exude a complex combination of self-reliance and vulnerability through spectacular displays of idealised adorability (Balcerzak 2005, 54). They were often positioned as happy-go-lucky orphans pluckily navigating their way through life almost completely alone. Such behaviour fit neatly with the escapist fantasy Hollywood propagated to distract the nation from the hardships resulting from economic depression and war. By the mid-forties, children in cinema still served as symbols of good citizenship and national pride, but they relayed this less through spectacle and more squarely within the narrative conflicts of the plot as spirited but duty-bound children. Natalie Wood's career begins at the same time as this transition.

In her early films, Wood hints at a kind of child-woman character in which the young girl possesses such emotional and intellectual maturity that, if not guided carefully, could lead to either greatness or destruction – of society as much as the self. Children were the objects of increased state and medical scrutiny as the government sought to build what Beth Bailey calls 'a national system of culture': a set of public strictures and expectations for the conduct of private life, including marriage, family and child care (1988, 7). Hollywood was firmly entrenched in this process, offering aspirational and indexical templates of what childhood could mean for the nation (O'Connor 2008, 3). In other words, Hollywood presupposed an imaginary of the child that legitimated the adult world (Lury 2010, 10). Building a nation around visions of prosperity, productivity and domestic stability altered conceptions of childhood from the Dickensian waif to a more socially aware child who could shepherd the traditional family into modern life (Sammond 2005, 193).

The story of how Wood became an actor mingles exemplary darlingness with technical proficiency and Old World quaintness. How much of it is true is not as important as how often the tale was repeated. In 1943, while visiting a film set on location in Santa Rosa, five-year-old Natasha Gurdin walked up to the director, Irving Pichel, climbed up on his lap and began to sing him a song. Enchanted, he gave her an uncredited scene at the beginning of the film. He also apparently asked her parents if he could adopt her and implored them to never 'spoil' the child by bringing her to Hollywood. Neither request was granted. The less charitable version of this story has Wood's mother, Maria Gurdin, an imperious Russian immigrant who passed herself off as a relative of the Romanoffs, rehearsing Wood's effort to seduce the director, teaching her an old-fashioned curtsey and training her how exactly to perform this act of childlike cuteness without annoying the adult with any un-cute childish behaviour. When the family uprooted to Hollywood in 1944, Gurdin pestered Pichel to give her daughter a screen test for his next film, the wartime melodrama *Tomorrow Is Forever*. The first attempt, at which the five-year-old was expected to cry on cue, was a disaster. Mindful of her obligation to be polite, poised and charming at all times, she simply refused to misbehave by crying in front of an adult. Upon discovering this, her mother was beside herself and badgered Pichel for a retake. It was then that Wood received her first acting lesson, from her sister Olga, who was herself studying Stanislavsky at drama classes. She recommended recalling a sad event, such as when she was younger and saw her dog get run over and killed by a car. With that image firmly planted, Wood sobbed so wretchedly that the director was delighted and her career was launched (Lambert 2004, 30; Moore 1984a, 21). Suzanne Finstad proposes a less charitable version of this story, claiming that her mother ripped a butterfly apart before the horrified child's eyes, invoking the hysteria and ensuring that Wood would never disobey a director again (2001, 38).

Later in life, Wood recalled, 'From that time on [after the screen test], whenever I did a movie, I always counted the crying scenes. That was a barometer of how difficult the part was going to be for me' (Moore 1984a, 22). It also became a hallmark of her acting. Wood was barely five feet tall and less than one hundred pounds as an adult. She lacked any real singing or dancing talent. While actors such as Shirley Temple are remembered for their bouncy hair, chubby legs and dimpled smile, Wood is remembered for her static unremarkableness, and her tears. As the powerful columnist Hedda Hopper recalled,

She wore Levi's and sweaters, and stood out from other screen tots, many of them bleached, permamented, and beruffled. On screen she has a direct and simple approach, and she could cry in a way that tore your heart (Hopper 1955, 22).

In *Tomorrow Is Forever*, Wood has six important scenes and sobs passionately in two of them. Playing against the towering Orson Welles, it is no insignificant feat that the tiny child of five is able to maintain her presence on screen as the war orphan Margaret Ludwig. This stock weepie is a vehicle for Claudette Colbert. She plays a woman with an infant son who is widowed during World War I. She remarries a wealthy industrialist who raises her son as his own. When war breaks out again, her first husband returns in disguise as a badly disfigured Austrian scientist with a young orphan, the child of the doctor who saved his life. Eventually Elizabeth (Colbert) realises that Erich Kessler (Welles) is in fact her husband John but not before he convinces her to put aside her own fears and allow their son to join the army. When she visits his home to thank him for releasing her from her haunted past, she discovers that he has died in the night and she takes the young girl home to be raised as her own daughter.

Pichel commented on Wood's ability to remain both childlike and suggest the woman-to-be underneath in the film. He said she possessed 'the sensitivity, the temperament, the understanding of that cross between child and adult – the *actress*' (Finstad 2001, 44). Such a definition presumes that a girl's maturity depends on her ability to sublimate deep psychological angst into an appropriately feminine sense of familial and national duty. Wood's Margaret certainly represents an idealised child, traumatised by geopolitical atrocities but not so badly that she cannot be a good and willing helper to the adults around her. Throughout the film, Wood uses her eyes to project a complex array of emotions. They could suddenly well up in a frenzy of tears, and just as quickly those tears would disappear and be replaced with a fixed stare indicating a host of repressed emotions. In an early scene introducing her character, she stands with Kessler waiting to have their immigration approved. He drops his hat and she quietly bends down to pick it up and hand it back to him before reclasping his hand, all without breaking her gaze. It is a superb piece of actorly business, so small is she in the frame, behind a large desk and beside a bear of a man, yet because of her eyes, all attention becomes focused on her. Later in the film, Margaret is frightened by the sound of a firecracker and begins to sob hysterically. Her guardian takes her on his knee and gives a speech – half to her, half to his son who does not know his identity but all for the audience's edification – about how she is the future of society and therefore must always be brave and do good work. With one gulp the tears stop and she apologises gravely for her outburst.

With Wood in the role, Margaret's relationship with Kessler hints at a more ambiguous (and fraught) sexuality than would be possible for the spectacularly white and innocent Shirley Temple. She is more wife and nursemaid than daughter, caring for Kessler and sublimating her own fears. This adult–child dynamic is typical in many postwar films where the young girl takes on a platonic heterosexual romance role with a strong, patriarchal surrogate. It is not the same as a Lolita-type relationship, but something far more complex (and maybe even more disturbing than the explicitly immoral sexuality of Nabokov's creation). The surrogate father does not secretly desire the child sexually as much as he prepares her for her sexual future as a wife and mother (Lury 2010, 57). In the immediate aftermath of World War II, that future was the foundation of a new social unit, the efficient, civic-minded nuclear family (Moran 2000, 133). Yet the traumas of world wars were far from over, and Wood's role as a war orphan compromises her status as innocent child. Safe from the ravages of war, Margaret's struggle comes from within, signified by her eyes. Her moments of tears are also moments when she must realise her responsibility to future generations and sublimate any psychic darkness back into acceptable

Natalie Wood and Orson Welles in *Tomorrow Is Forever* (1946) (RKO/Photofest)

levels of desirability and maturity. It is not surprising, then, that one of the first movie fan-magazine tributes to the little actress, released even before *Tomorrow Is Forever* debuted, called her a 'Six-Year-Old Siren' (in Finstad 2001, 45). This darkness-infused sublimated sexuality is an aspect of Wood's stardom that helped her progress into adult roles and is discussed in greater detail in Chapter 3.

    Tomorrow Is Forever opened to solid reviews and strong box office. Her next film, also for Pichel, was the forgettable romp *The Bride Wore Boots* (1946). Although the film failed to capture an audience, Wood's reputation as a dutiful, pliant actress brought her to the attention of Twentieth Century-Fox, who signed her to a seven-year contract in 1947 after she appeared in two of their prestige films. She played Gene Tierney's young daughter Anna in *The Ghost and Mrs. Muir* (1947), a small and largely insignificant performance especially since the most important scene for the daughter is played by another actress as the grown-up Anna. At the same time as shooting that film in California, she was also on set in New York for *Miracle on 34th Street*. In it she plays Susan Walker, the sombre and precocious child of Doris, a divorced career woman played by Maureen O'Hara. Doris works in the promotional department at Macy's and they live in a highrise apartment in Manhattan where a handsome and kindly neighbour ingratiates himself into their lives with the help of a jolly soul by the name of Kris Kringle (Edmund Gwynn). Raised to reject fairytales, imagination and Santa Claus, Susan only agrees to let herself be a child if her one wish is granted: a Cape Cod home in Long Island. Together the smitten neighbour, Fred Gailey (John Payne), and Kris Kringle conspire to teach mother and child how to perform their feminine roles correctly, and thus be rewarded with the American Dream.

There is no crying in *Miracle on 34th Street*. Instead, Wood's performance depends on her sceptical gaze on the adults surrounding her as they debate what's right for a child until ultimately her cynicism gives way to boundless joy and the return of innocence. Thus, several pivotal scenes hinge on close-ups of Wood. At Macy's, Fred takes Susan to see Kris – working as the department store Santa – against Doris's wishes. Susan is nonplussed and looks unnervingly at the 'silly' adults. But her icy stare turns to astonishment when she witnesses Kris speaking Dutch to an orphan refugee, a little girl who looks a bit like Susan herself. As the camera jumps back and forth between the happy duo and a silent Susan lurking nearby, it is evident that the scepticism has all but disappeared and the little girl is ready to believe. It is now up to the

Natalie Wood and Edmund Gwynn in *Miracle on 34th Street* (1947) (20th Century Fox/Photofest)

mother to prove once again that there is no Santa Claus, no magic wishes and no fairytale endings – especially for girls. Her bitterness causes Kris to conspire with Fred, 'Those two are a couple of lost souls. It's up to us to help them.'

Both men begin their self-assigned task by focusing on Susan. Kris decides to teach Susan how to play like a child by encouraging her to pretend to be a monkey. As in the department store, Susan moves from scepticism to wonder as she awkwardly starts prancing around the room scratching and grunting. The stilted and not quite successful attempt is more evidence of her natural rather than spectacular charm. One can hardly imagine Shirley Temple not instantly springing to life and executing the most dazzlingly perfect monkey imaginable. Susan then entrusts Kris with her secret dream to move out of their apartment and live in a real house 'with a great big tree to put a swing on' in the backyard. She lies still in bed with the covers up over her with her face in close-up. As her voice rises excitedly when she describes her dream home, her eyes widen and dart about, eyelashes fluttering. After Kris tucks her in, the film lingers on Susan as she practises blowing bubbles and snapping her gum, again revealing her natural instincts to be a child, which have been repressed by the unnatural environment provided by her mother.

Later that night, Fred confesses his own wish for a house, 'Not a big place, just one of those junior partner deals around Manhasset', a bedroom community on the North Shore of Long Island that to this day is considered a haven for young families. The film concludes with them all in a car, lost in Long Island, when they suddenly find themselves in front of the exact same house that Susan had shown Kris. At this instance she is finally a child, scampering around the house, calling her mother 'Mommy', and racing out to the backyard to try the swing. Fred realises that Doris does love him and they decide to buy the house. This conclusion, a real-estate transaction, not an actual marriage proposal, speaks to the importance of the suburbs in the postwar American imagination (Harris 2007). It also makes the fact that the child in the film is a girl all the more significant. Only a girl could be satisfied with a retreat to the suburbs. Furthermore, the kind of actor who can make this transformation believable cannot be known for her 'spectacularness'. She must be ordinary and childlike in order to fit into this environment. Of course, the suburbs were far from natural, being carefully planned as a buffer between the competing ideals of modern, progressive urbanism and traditional ruralism. It was the idealised child who made the suburbs appear as natural. The child's place in the suburbs was the focal point between two conflicting visions of America, one sentimentally nostalgic and the other ruthlessly futuristic. In that sense, then, the presence of the child reconnects the rural to the urban, making the suburbs appear authentically American rather than socially engineered (Sammond 2005, 21).

It was actually rare at this time for a film featuring a child to be located in a major city, particularly if the film was set in contemporary times. Baltimore is the setting for *Tomorrow Is Forever* and New York for *Miracle on 34th Street*. However, both films rectify their incongruency by concluding with the child's removal from an inner-city apartment into a leafy suburb. Wood's next three films all had rural settings but none had the prestige backing of her previous efforts, and in them Wood was typecast as the no-nonsense child who helps guide the adults to their rightful destinies. For her eighth film since *Tomorrow Is Forever*, Wood was loaned out to a private company funded by Houston oil tycoon Glenn McCarthy to play yet another kid sister in a rural family in *The Green Promise*. He wanted to produce a film that would explicitly extol the virtues of modern American rural identity, with particular emphasis on agricultural science and national social programmes like the 4-H Club. While the other two films discussed in this chapter can be claimed to present their social message obliquely and perhaps even only subconsciously, *The Green Promise* was a very deliberate piece of movie propaganda. With her pigtails-and-play-clothes image, Wood was an ideal choice for the dutiful but feisty daughter who teaches her cantankerous father, played by Walter Brennan, the true values of American farming. The film not only marks a transformation in farming but also in the family, as an elderly widower sets himself and his four children on a path to financial and emotional ruin with his stubborn adherence to traditional farming methods and domineering parenting style. He is slowly usurped as the patriarch by the county agricultural supervisor, David Barkley, played by the ruggedly handsome Robert Paige, who romantically pursues the eldest daughter, Deborah Matthews (Marguerite Chapman).

Like Fred in *Miracle on 34th Street*, David first ingratiates himself with the youngest child in the family, Susan, played by Wood. These relationships hark back to the more explicit dynamic in *Tomorrow Is Forever*, as the child-woman is trained by a paternal romantic figure to desire a nuclear family. The fact that Paige was thirty-nine and Chapman thirty to Wood's ten, and that Brennan characteristically looks much older than his fifty-five years, creates a generational sleight-of-hand in the film. The eldest sister is already old enough to be Susan's mother (who is presumably dead but never really mentioned). Brennan's Mr Matthews (he's never given a first name) is more of a grandfather role and an exemplar of how adherence to tradition will stand in the way of America's prosperity. David is established as the man who will rescue the community from the ignorance of men like Matthews. However, the task before him will not be an easy one. Unable to make Deborah break with her father, and with the other children so cowed that they can only obey him timidly or try to curry favour by acting as his spy when the other members of the family step out of line, David goes to the only person left for whom there is still hope: Susan. He tells her, 'You may be the key to let the sunshine in.' He takes her under his wing to show her firsthand what opportunities are available for young children ready to embrace new methods and mindsets. Travelling the county with him, Susan discovers her independence from her father through both a new farming venture, raising sheep through the 4-H Club, and a new romantic venture, a spirited relationship with the head of her local club, Buzz Wexford (Robert Ellis).

The conflation of whiteness with the American ideal underlies this film too. At a masquerade party hosted by local 4-H wonderkid and Susan's budding love interest, Buzz, she is positioned between a plump young girl dressed as a Mammy with kerchief and minstrelsy blackface, her wretchedly devious sister Abigail (Connie Marshall) in an exotic Suzy Wong costume and Buzz's little sister Jessie (Jeanne LaDuke) as Mata Hari in a belly-dance outfit and veil. Susan herself

is dressed as a snow-white bunny, standing out starkly against the other dark costumes even as she is dwarfed by the other actresses in ways that emphasise her natural purity and innocence. As the child who best exemplifies the characteristics of whiteness, Susan is also romantically – albeit innocently, of course – linked to Buzz Wexford. He unabashedly confesses his crush on her by asking her to be his date to his party, letting her help care for his prize bull and showing her how to pump the organ (a rare piece of physical humour from Wood as she pumps so vigorously that the handle breaks off and sends her flying across the room). Thus, within the film, even more than the eldest sister, Susan exemplifies the virtues of modern American womanhood. She is presented as a mother to her lambs; a wife-in-training to a successful, modern farmer boy; and an industrious worker who channels her gendered desires into suitable labour that will ultimately benefit the whole family. As in the other films discussed here, the future of the family and the nation rests squarely on Wood's tiny shoulders. Her ability to convey naturalness, subtly coded by a racialised performance to underscore her feminine pliancy and sexual purity, became a hallmark of her child roles.

Wood's teen and adult success built upon her childlike persona. Even in adulthood, Wood's body never quite matured and so the child within was always readily apparent. She remained throughout her career the 'six-year-old siren' – erotic yet innocent. She embodied a series of contradictory attitudes and stances that redefined the ingénue for a more psychologically tinged era: spirited yet docile, independent and mature yet respectful of her elders, progressive yet conventional, unremarkable yet with an emotional intensity beyond her years. As she grew up on screen, some critics remarked that they could still see traces of the 'child-woman' within (Benner 1988, 31; Lyle 1964, 94). Thus, by way of conclusion, I want to briefly discuss her role as Debbie in *The Searchers* (1956). Although small, it is arguably her most significant transitional role from child to woman, as well as being her first racial 'passing' role.

Filmed immediately after Wood had wrapped *Rebel Without a Cause* and graduated from high school, *The Searchers* marks her transition from child to teenager even more than the former film. When her character is first introduced, she is a little girl (played by her younger sister, Lana Wood). The adolescent Debbie as played by Natalie Wood doesn't appear until about eighty minutes into the film. Widely considered one of the greatest Westerns ever made, *The Searchers* examines postwar trauma, race, sex, rugged individualism and scarred psychology through the comfortable distance of nineteenth-century frontierism (Buscombe 2000). When Comanche warriors attack a frontier community, Civil War veteran Ethan Edwards (John Wayne) embarks on a crusade of revenge and rescue. His brother is killed, as is his sister-in-law, Martha (Dorothy Jordan), whom Edwards secretly loves. Their daughters are missing so a posse sets out to find them. Edwards finds the eldest daughter's raped body but the youngest child, Debbie, is still missing. Five years pass, and the search party whittles down to only him and Martin (Jeffrey Hunter), an orphan raised by his brother despite being one-eighth Cherokee. When they finally discover Debbie as one of the Comanche chief's wives, Edwards and Martin begin to feud over whether she can be returned home or if she's now 'one of them'. That tension builds right up to the moment that Edwards chases

Debbie down, while the reformed posse raids the Comanche village. As he dismounts to strike her dead, a drastic change of heart overcomes Edwards. Instead he lifts her up just as he did when she was a little girl at the beginning of the film and says, 'Let's go home, Debbie.' They return to the settlement and Debbie is brought into a neighbour's home. Edwards, however, lingers outside the door, which, in one of the most famous shots in American cinema, slowly closes on him – domesticated, at peace America no longer has room for heroes like Ethan Edwards.

Wood has very little to do in the film, other than react. It is very much John Wayne's film and Debbie is 'merely the object of the search' (ibid., 58). Thus, it is worth wondering why Warners put their newest hot teen property back into pigtails. Wood herself felt miserably miscast but, while there is little in the way of character development, Wood's dark colouring, expressive eyes and unthreateningly petite frame made her ideally suited to play a child-woman dangerously criss-crossing the thresholds of both racial purity and sexual maturity. Earlier in the film, Edwards and Martin find some white women rescued from a Comanche tribe. Although they are all blonde and blue-eyed, they have gone insane from the sexual abuse they endured, so much so that Edwards deems them no longer white. When they finally find Debbie, she looms over them steadily holding a pole with the scalp of her mother. Unlike the crazed women from before, she meets their gaze steadily and knowingly, with only a flicker of fear. She is dressed in generic Hollywood native garb, with her braids no longer signifying innocence but racial pollution. Her gaudy make-up – heavy eyeliner and bright orangey-red lipstick – confuses both her sexual and racial identity. Is she a child or a woman? Glamorously white or savagely native? Neither the other female lead, Vera Miles as Hunter's love interest, nor the other traumatised white women wear such heavy make-up. Wood alone is styled so brazenly. With her role almost exclusively reaction shots to either Wayne or Hunter, those kohl-covered eyes do most of the

The Searchers (1956) (Warner Bros./Photofest)

work. Wayne commented on Wood's ability to meet his legendary steely stare and give so much through eye contact alone, and Ford relied heavily on close-ups to convey all the fear, hope, desire and loss in a girl who depends on an uncle-father to either restore her innocence or destroy her altogether (Finstad 2001, 200).

By the time *The Searchers* was released, James Dean had become a macabre legend and Wood was on her way to teen stardom. She barely acknowledged the film in the press, preferring to be known more for her social life than her acting. Fan magazines called her 'date bait' (1956) and 'a lady on the loose' (Lane 1956). One journalist commented with frustration:

Contradictory, puzzling, willful, exciting, she is walking a chalk line between adolescence and maturity. And no one – not even Natalie – can predict which minute she will choose to be a woman and which minute she will choose to be a bothersome elf (Meltsir 1956, 21).

With the press alternately bemused and infuriated by her, and a studio unsure of its next move, Wood's career was on shaky ground. Yet, as director (and rumoured lover) Nicholas Ray insisted,

In spite of the fact that the transition from child actress to ingénue is a very difficult step and the odds are usually against anyone being able to make it, it seemed to me that Natalie was the one who could do the part [of Judy in *Rebel Without a Cause*] – and also show the most promise for the picture and the studio (Ott 1956, 105).

His prediction proved correct as, under the controlling influence of Method actors and directors, Wood achieved her greatest acting successes.

2 THE SEXUAL HYSTERIC

Like many child actors before her, Wood's career sputtered to a halt
around the age of twelve. She rebooted it in her teens by signing with
agent Henry Willson in 1954, who arranged a series of publicity
dates with his roster of 'beefcake' actors, including Tab Hunter, Troy
Donahue and Rock Hudson. Most of Willson's clients were closeted
gay men and some speculate that Wood was used as a 'beard'. Wood
understood this but didn't care, as it got her name in the magazines
(Finstad 2001, 158). Her entrée into Hollywood society at the age of
sixteen came on the precipice of an explosive youth culture,
buttressed by new theories of children as self-aware adults in
training. Girls, especially, needed to be guided through the
treacherous terrain of sexuality, ensuring they pass through all proper
stages of development and emerge as 'healthy' and 'normal' adults.
The expectation was explicitly framed as heterosexual, middle-class
(in affectation if not necessarily in economics) and sexually aware –
but not so aware as to be promiscuous and risk turning into a 'sexual
delinquent' – a term only used to describe girls (Scheiner 2000, 7).
As famed sociologist Talcott Parsons insisted, girls developed in
accordance with family roles and an understanding that they would
be primarily responsible not for the economic maintenance of a
household, as in eras past, but for the psychological maintenance of
husband, children and then, lastly, themselves. Divergence from that
path signalled a problem with their development (1963, 133).

Hollywood was quick to recognise the rising trend of a youth-obsessed culture. By the mid-fifties, it was facing serious threats to its dominance both globally, as European countries began to rebuild their film industries, and domestically, as television cut into its profits. In the ten years following World War II, studio contracts, the bulwark of the industry, shrank to approximately 25 per cent of their previous totals, while feature-film production dropped 50 per cent by the end of the 1950s (Langford 2010, 24). Under these tense economic conditions, studios sought out neglected or niche audiences. Thus, teenagers became a lucrative market. What some called 'an aimless, incoherent mass of contradictory consumption trends', others called a goldmine (Douvan and Adelson 1966, 229). Increasingly defined as a homogenous, highly privileged social demographic, which transcended racial and class demarcations in pursuit of unbridled freedom and pleasure, teens represented the consumer ethos of the American Dream (Doherty 1988, 46; Loizidou 2005, 195). They were, therefore, at once a 'mass' and 'niche' audience who could potentially deliver huge profits to Hollywood and render the film industry relevant again.

Attracting a teen market was only possible by offering it what television did not – sharply observant, hard-hitting stories about their everyday anxieties, elevated to crisis levels. Herbert Gans called these 'social problem films' and highlighted the importance of teenagers to this genre:

The problems of being an adolescent in America: how to achieve adulthood, how to cope with the social and emotional contradictions of teenage status, and how to deal with sexual urges are considered in many films, and are acted out by the youngsters who have suddenly become Hollywood's biggest stars (1964, 331).

Aiding and abetting this transformation was a growing fascination with the Method style of acting and directing, which, when translated from theatrical stage to cinematic screen, lost none of its emotional cacophony. Technological achievements in colour and widescreen formats provided the expansive landscape for the adolescent social-problem film, heightening the hyperbolic obsession with women's virtue that already characterised Hollywood melodrama (Leibman 1995, 17). Two of Wood's most significant films, *Rebel Without a Cause* and *Splendor in the Grass*, are often cited as hallmarks of the adolescent social-problem film' and of Hollywood's flirtations with Method. Yet Wood herself is rarely acknowledged as the star of these and many other films of the late fifties and early sixties that scoped the territory of young women's burgeoning sexuality. The reason, I would suggest, has to do with the swaggering neurotic masculinity inherent in the most celebrated of Method actors, her own lack of formal Method training, her wavering between the desire to be treated as a serious actress and as a glamorous star and the sexual revolution quickly undoing this cloistered, conservative vision of containable female sexuality.

Nina Leibman and Susan Douglas have recuperated from cinematic history what I here call the virgin melodrama (Douglas calls them pregnancy melodramas although not all of them deal with accidental pregnancies) (Douglas 1994, 73; Leibman 1987, 1995). Leibman notes that in these films,

The central moral dilemma was thus no longer whether a woman could defend her virtue (or, more commonly, have it defended for her) but whether she was (or should be) virtuous to begin with, and more important, whether the proper expression for her chastity should be as the domestic heart of the nuclear household (1995, 17).

Indeed, both *Rebel* and *Splendour* – not to mention lesser-known films like *A Cry in the Night* (1956), *Marjorie Morningstar* or the racial passing films discussed in the following chapter (*Kings Go Forth, All the Fine Young Cannibals* and, of course, *West Side Story*) – offer little more conflict and resolution for Wood's characters than a brief dalliance with sexual promiscuity that usually results in madness (for her and/or the characters around her), followed by her capitulation to either passionless marriage or martyred singledom. This chapter examines Wood as the hysterical ingénue, and her centrality to adolescent social-problem films for a fleeting moment between the early fifties' culture of containment and the sexual revolutions of the sixties. This role was best realised in her most Method-influenced films – not coincidentally also two of the most commercial and critical successes of her career.

Rebel Without a Cause is often cited as *the* social-problem film, portraying teenage angst as the single most important issue affecting America. The film follows a day in the life of Jim Stark (James Dean), his new girlfriend Judy (Wood) and his adoring friend Plato (Sal Mineo), as they stare down death, loneliness and their parents on their way from delinquency to sexual maturity. *Splendor in the Grass* sprawls across a generation as two star-crossed lovers risk madness and ruin only to realise that they're better off without each other. In both cases, Wood plays 'the wholesome sex girl' at odds with her desires, desperately seeking a man who will take control of them for her (Hull 1959, B6). Wood succeeds in these roles because of her ability to convey both profound emotions through the limitless depths of her dark eyes, and vulnerability via through the childlike fragility of her tiny body. Her voice, thin and tight, would suddenly escape into a roar of frustrated emotions made larger-than-life by close-ups that zeroed in on her eyes. Her Method directors, Nicholas Ray and his own mentor Elia Kazan, delighted in her malleability and largely took credit for the performances they wrung from her with Svengali-like glee.

When Wood first learned of the role of Judy in *Rebel Without a Cause*, she was an unsigned, unemployed actress attending a regular public high school and hanging out with rising bad boy actor Nick Adams (who had a small role in the film as one of the delinquents).

She credits this part not only for rescuing her career, but also as a transformative experience in her life. Wood saw *Rebel Without a Cause* as a chance to assert her independence from both family and studio bosses, and gain access to a privileged inner circle of Hollywood that was just beginning to form:

'My decision to do "Rebel Without a Cause" was one of the most critical decisions in my life,' she says now. 'Up until then I hadn't taken acting seriously. I'd allowed studios and my parents to guide my life and career. I played in 'Rebel' against my parents' advice. It was my first decision as an adult. I guess I was rebelling against being over-protected. I hated being constantly hovered over at the studio and being treated like a child' (Cuskelly 1974, E2).

The title of the film came from a brief psychological treatise written by Dr Robert Lindner about using hypnotherapy to treat psychopaths. Warner Bros. optioned the book and passed it to a series of directors and screenwriters before handing it to up-and-coming director Nicholas Ray. Keeping only the title, Ray transformed the story into one of middle-class teenagers raised in the Hollywood Hills, estranged from their emotionally repressed parents and therefore forced to grow up on their own. When lonely misfit Jim Stark comes to town, he gets on the wrong side of 'the kids', a group of rebellious hooligans who dare Jim to a 'chicki-ride'. Things go horribly wrong when Buzz (Corey Allen), the leader of the gang, drives off a cliff. Jim is hunted by the rest of the gang members and he hides out in an abandoned mansion with his only friend, Plato, and Buzz's girlfriend Judy. There, they embark on a fantasy of family security before both the gang and the police violently disrupt them. Plato is killed, and Jim, with Judy at his side, decides to reconcile with his family.

Ray was deeply committed to *Rebel Without a Cause* and aggressively courted the then-unknown New York-based actor, James

Dean for the lead role of Jim Stark. However, he had no one specific actress in mind for Judy and agreed to a succession of screen tests to find someone who would meet his exacting standards. The role would be tricky to fill as Ray had very clear ideas of how she should look, act and feel. In his original screenplay treatment, Ray drew a picture of Judy as a girl deep in the throes of her own erotic confusion:

Occasionally you run across a Barbara Hutton or Judy Garland at this age who gives the feeling that she doesn't know where she's going but she's on her way. She is ebullient, giving, a center of attention, a girl who is living for the moment – 'having a ball' – when she is away from home.

At home she is lipstickless, appealing, docile, demure. She is also critical of her mother when her father is not around, and filled with adoration for the father who has all of the positive qualities with none of the economic burdens of Johnny in 'Tree Grows in Brooklyn.' Judy considers him an Adonis with the humor of Joe E. Lewis and the voice of Perry Como. Whatever she does, she does to get the attention of her father.

So she is a girl who has not caught up with reality and has found no satisfaction in any of her promiscuous relations with boys her own age, nor enough attention in her family relationships to give her any satisfaction. She begins to mature with Jimmy, at which point she is pure as Juliet – sharp as Hutton (Ray in USC Warner Bros. Archives, 13 December 1954).

Ray's detailed description – far more detailed than those for Jimmy or Plato – envisioned a girl on the precipice of an adolescent rebellion defined almost exclusively by confusion between love and lust, first for her father then for the father-figure lover, Jimmy. Sex would simultaneously be her downfall and her redemption. Thus, finding an actress who could be believable as both a virginal sweetheart and a promiscuous rebel was crucial to the film. Judy had to be played by someone with whom he could be close – as it turns out, perhaps too close. The casting process for the male gang members was largely physical, as Ray would provoke them into fights to see how long they could maintain high levels of testosterone-fuelled angst. The girls, however, were brought into his office for private chats about their family relationships and other invasive questions (Frascella and Weisel 2005, 72).

Dean, who was working with Elia Kazan on *East of Eden* (1955), wanted as his co-star Carroll Baker, an Actors Studio veteran who went on to star in Kazan's follow-up film, *Baby Doll* (1956). Ray was keen to cast her but her husband became jealous of her friendships with Dean and Ray and she dutifully declined the role (Baker 1983, 99). The studio is said to have recommended Jayne Mansfield, but Ray refused to even consider her. He wanted Judy to be more girl-next-door than jail-bait. Debbie Reynolds, under contract with MGM, was suggested, but Ray felt she was too old (she was one year younger than Dean and the same age as Ray's first choice, Baker). Ray approached Margaret O'Brien, Wood's good friend, who was also struggling to reignite her acting career, but she apparently blew her audition by speaking lovingly about her parents. Ray didn't want a good girl who liked being a good girl, he wanted one who was ready to break out and be bad. Then Natalie Wood entered his office, dressed to the nines, wearing too much make-up, wobbly heels and glittering jewellery in a comically pathetic attempt to appear sophisticated. He was nonplussed but did notice Nick Adams waiting for her in the hallway, a tough-looking boy, the kind parents don't want around their daughters. Later, on the advice of friends, she ambushed Ray at the Warners commissary, this time dressed more like a bobby soxer than a femme fatale. He asked about her friend, Nick Adams, and eventually cast him as one of the gang members. He then invited Wood to his bungalow at the Chateau Marmont, and they began a sexual affair, but he still refused to give her the coveted role (Frascella and Weisel 2005, 34; Sheppard 1988, 8).

The legendary story of how Wood ultimately clinched the part has been told many times, including by the actress herself. After an evening of joy riding with Dennis Hopper, they crashed the car and were rushed to the hospital. Rather than call her parents, Wood insisted they call Ray. He rushed to her bedside where she pointed at a doctor and said, 'He called me a goddamn juvenile delinquent. Now do I get the part?' (Ott 1956, 105). Ray was convinced but the studio was still resistant. He took it upon himself to transform her physically and emotionally into the complex character of Judy. He hired a movement coach to bring a hint of sexual titillation to her walk and a vocal coach to remove the high-pitched squeak in her voice. Her hair and make-up were altered to appear more natural. With Moss Mabrey, a studio costume designer, Ray refashioned Wood's body, padding her stick-thin boyish figure into a demure hourglass. He then wrote to the studio heads and encouraged them to sign her:

Keeping in mind that whatever known qualities possessed by the actors involved in the test were ignored, in the same way that little attention was paid to makeup or wardrobe, there is only one girl who has shown the capacity to play Judy, and she is Natalie Wood (Ray in USC Warner Bros. Archives 1 March 1955).

Wood was so desperate for the part and eager to remain involved in this new scene of intense New York actors at the hedonistic Chateau Marmont that she recalls blurting out to Jack Warner in the midst of contract negotiations, 'I'd do this part for nothing!' She very nearly got her wish. The seventeen-year-old actor, who had been the sole breadwinner for her family for much of her childhood, was signed to a seven-year contract with Warners for $400 a week, half her starting salary with Fox eight years earlier (Finstad 2001, 178).

With his cast assembled, Ray often brought them together in his bungalow at the Chateau Marmont for improvisational sessions, script readings and other actorly exercises. Dean was a peripatetic soul, drifting in and out, sometimes using the door, sometimes the window. Wood, self-consciously attired in high heels and tight clothing, clung to the side of her director-and-secret-lover. It was, in fact, not a very well-kept secret. Fan magazines such as *Photoplay* and *Movieland* featured photos of her on dates with Ray and commented on her penchant for older men. 'Older men make her feel older … and her greatest longing is to portray girls older than herself' (Block 1956, 112). Susan Strasberg recalls seeing Wood lounging poolside at the Marmont, heavily made-up and smoking a cigarette. 'That's what I want to be like when I'm older,' she remembers thinking, even though they were around the same age (Frascella and Weisel 2005, 142). This arch sophistication was dispelled once shooting began and Wood was required to play what she herself was: a lonely, mixed-up kid desperate to grow up.

Wood often commented in the press on her desire to play roles that meshed with her own experiences, sometimes to the point of losing sight of where her identity ended and the character's began. It was not that she was looking for her art to imitate her life, but that she deliberately chose to play characters whose feelings were akin to her own. As she once said of the role of Judy, 'You can't pinpoint what it is that draws you to a character, you just say I know her, I know about her or I just feel that I can make her real' ('Hollywood and the Stars' 1964). Later, she clarified, 'I loved Judy and I felt very much of a connection, an identification with the part. I guess I was going through my first rebellion' (Lawford 1975). *Rebel Without a Cause* became an important film for Wood not only because it was her first 'grown-up' role, but also because it transformed her acting. Film commentators noticed:

In *Rebel*, Natalie found a new approach to acting. She went into more detail than she had ever done before – relating the part to herself, making it real to herself. … [said Ray] 'They weren't playing effect or result. They were playing from the inside out' (Ott 1956, 106).

With director Nicholas Ray on the set of
Rebel Without a Cause (1955) (BFI)

Up until then, acting was the work she did to be a star; now acting took on a significance of its own, at times conflicting with her other ambition to be a glamorous Hollywood star.

Ray relied on techniques learned from Kazan and the Group Theater, and to a lesser extent Strasberg's Actors Studio. Many have mentioned his particular emphasis on improvisation, although as Stewart Stern, the screenwriter, notes, there was in fact very little divergence from the shooting script (Baer 1999, np). It appears that improvisation came more in movement, blocking and setting, and through exercises run by Ray to make the actors – especially the young gang members – comfortable with each other. The three leads kept somewhat to themselves – Dean because he felt that was true to his character, Wood and Mineo because they were minors under the strict supervision of their on-set tutor and guardian. Still, Wood was exposed to a world of acting far removed from Hollywood traditions. Ray coaxed – sometimes ruthlessly – an emotional performance that only occasionally veered back to her childhood tricks of maudlin tears and screeching vocals. She claimed that Ray (and later, Kazan):

changed the course of my professional life. Nick introduced me to a new way of working, doing improvisations. It opened the door to a whole new world; it was just glorious. Here were things that I had never dreamt of – improvising, motion memory, sense memory, attending classes, going to the Actors Studio in New York, perhaps even doing theatre. All this was just incredible to me (Moore 1984a, 173).

As the film was shot more or less in sequence, it is possible to watch Wood's acting grow in confidence. The brittleness of her portrayal, initially a reaction to her anxiety and insecurity around Dean and Ray, slowly pays off as both Wood the actor and Judy the character come into their own.

Ray and Stern decided to play up a quasi-incestuous relationship between Judy and her father to underscore her desperate search for love. There is some confusion over her sexual status in the film. Stern has made conflicting comments about wanting Judy to be promiscuous as evidence of her loneliness and estrangement from her father, but also wanting the film to eventually reveal that both she and Jim are virgins (Frascella and Weisel 2005, 167). Of course, the Production Code Office made no bones about the fact that Judy must be (and remain) a virgin and that there be no incestuous overtones to her relationship with her father. In a pivotal scene with Judy's family, her brash bravado is gone along with her lipstick as she leans forward to get a kiss from her father. He rebuffs her, gently at first, then slaps her hard, sending her off into the night to seek love elsewhere. The day that scene was shot, Wood recalls, 'four executives with briefcases showed up on the set' to ensure that the kiss landed on the cheek and not the mouth (Clein 1970, 8). Five days after shooting began, the head of the Production Code, Geoffrey Shurlock, sent a warning about the 'element of illicit sex' present in the final shooting script, highlighting all of Judy's major scenes: her police station interview after being caught walking the streets alone at night; her thwarted kiss with her father; her encounter with Jim after Buzz is killed; and their gentle love scene in the abandoned mansion (PCA Files 31 March 1955). However, as was so often the case in the waning days of the Production Code, these admonishments became issues of interpretation, as everything they highlight as problematically suggestive remains in the final film. These scenes thus shed further light on the postwar cinematic tropes of teen-girl sexuality, which often relied on Electra-infused psychodramas that eventually sort themselves out once the girl finds a young man to whom she can transfer her masochistic need to be dominated by love.

The first shot of Judy is as a scarlet woman, dressed in a bright red coat and hat and wearing a slash of dark red lipstick. The red was chosen deliberately to signify Judy's questionable sexual behaviour, but the film gently subdues its intensity after each scene until, by the end of the film, Judy is in a soft powder pink and the passionate reds have transferred to Jim's jacket and Plato's sock. The detective asks her pointedly, 'You weren't looking for company, were you?' She cries in protest, as she speaks incoherently about how her father either ignores her or calls her 'a dirty tramp', and that 'I don't even know why I do it …'. Warner Bros. was so pleased with the rushes from this scene that they released a communiqué declaring that 'Natalie's crying scene equals a mark set by Bette Davis' ('Miss Wood Wins Praise of Director' 1955). What they didn't discuss, of course, was how terrifying this scene was to a young actor who had been brutalised into crying on cue throughout her childhood and who was desperate to prove herself to her emotionally controlling director.

Rebel Without a Cause

According to some of her castmates, Wood spent the morning agonising over the scene, when Ray, perhaps sensing her distress, called an early lunch. At that, she went into a frenzy and had to be carried off the set, kicking and screaming. She next tried to employ an old studio trick of dabbing Vicks under her eyes but Ray caught her and proceeded to eviscerate her in front of everyone. 'Ray accused her of being a bad actress and asked himself out loud, "How did I ever hire her?" Ray just ripped her apart and she started crying. And then he said, "OK, let's go"' (Frascella and Weisel 2005, 168). The result is a scene that certainly delivers hysteria but lacks emotional depth. She delivers all her lines mechanically in the same cadence and at the same medium volume. Her face contorts and real tears stream down her face but the Technicolor lighting makes her skin garish and the bright red costuming is distracting. Perhaps part of the reason why this scene fails to connect is the widescreen ratio that leaves too much empty space around Wood, even in close-up. Usually, close-ups work effectively for Wood as the camera can train right into her eyes. Instead, the gaze is drawn to her vulgarly red, twisted mouth as she keeps shouting her lines defiantly but not convincingly. Ray once stated that close-ups help 'as the actor moves from confusion to clarity to decision, or gets a new idea, or reveals something, or has something revealed to him' (1993, 82). Nothing of that emotional journey happens as Judy begins and ends a hysterical, confused child acting out against her father.

To Ray, Wood was no 'natural', like Dean or even Mineo. She needed coaxing and prodding, technical lessons and the occasional emotional manipulation to draw her character out from within her. He said of his method, '[it] requires a relationship between actor and director such that everything said between you, either in the preliminary contact or between takes, is of a terribly intimate nature in its content and associations' (ibid., 80). While the intimacy with Dean was one of two artists with a shared vision, with Wood it was far more controlling and manipulative. Wood was regarded by Ray as the type of actor who needed 'their bad habits broken without completely deflating their confidence' (ibid., 75). Having failed to achieve that balance in her first major scene, Ray now had the opportunity to try anew with the love scene between Judy and Jim in the abandoned mansion. Sensing Wood's anxiety over her first cinematic kiss, he admonished Dean to lay off the teasing and banished the rest of the cast and most of the crew from the set. Up until then, Wood admitted to focusing only on the mechanics of the kiss.

I felt like a fighter before a match – let's go in and get it over with. Jimmy was saying something, but all I could think of was 'Is this the way – should I do it the way I rehearsed? Maybe that was too smooth. Maybe I should fumble a little' (Wood 1955, 84).

Ray quietly coaxed her to relax and let herself melt into Dean and the camera. If anything, it is Dean who is nervous, mumbling interruptions like 'I'm glad' that add nothing to Judy's heartfelt confession that 'All the time I've been looking for someone to love me, and now I love somebody.' Ray closes the camera in tight this

Rebel Without a Cause

time, with Wood resting gently on top of Dean, her eyes wide open while his are closed.

For the first time in the film, Wood seems to convey emotion sincerely, rather than relying on tricks and volume. She is confident yet dreamy, existing in her own reverie – what Ray called an 'involuntary performance'. In an interview later in life, he explained:

After an involuntary performance the actor is kind of stunned and bewildered, he doesn't know what just happened to him. He is in shock at having caught sight of his own evasions, tricks, and clichés, or at sensing something of his own vast, untapped resources, or at being forced to question why he became an actor at all. At such moments, the director knows that he has found something, released something which nobody in the world could have told the actor was there (Ray 1993, 87).

While the whole love scene marks a turning point for Wood, the moment when Dean turns gently to meet her lips and her eyes flutter nervously for a moment before she presses down on him is a particular triumph. For perhaps the first time in her career, Wood let herself ignore the cameras and even her director – who had, in fact called 'Cut' just before realising that the performance he'd been

'Strange Doings of an Actress at Practice'.
Photographed by Ralph Crane for *Life* magazine
(1956) (Ralph Crane/The LIFE Picture
Collection/Getty Images)

waiting for was about to unfurl. Lawrence Frascella and Al Weisel, in their book on the making of the film, state that with this scene, unlike the more anxious-to-please performance in the police station 'she became a different kind of actress, far less studio-tooled, more daring and more mature' (2005, 169).

In the immediate years following the release of *Rebel*, Wood flirted with Method in the same way she flirted with Hollywood bachelors. She appears to be doing both in a fascinating photo-essay in *Life* magazine, 'The Strange Doings of an Actress at Practice' (1957, 97–100). Showcasing Wood with her perennial sidekicks, Nick Adams and Dennis Hopper, the feature marks a turning point in the way Hollywood presented its actors as skilled craftspersons. Baron and Carnicke define that transition as a shift away from 'mechanically reproduced instinctive behavior' to a more conscious and self-reflective method of inhabiting characters. In other words, the Hollywood studio system encouraged the belief that actors were merely portraying enlarged versions of themselves while the post-studio approach sought legitimacy for their stars based on their commitment to the craft of acting (2008, 24). In the most telling photo of the magazine spread, Wood leans over to discuss a scene from Elia Kazan's *A Streetcar Named Desire*, with Vivien Leigh's face looming over them. Both actresses' eyes are enormous, Leigh conveying confusion and terror while Wood demonstrates insight and understanding. If the intention of this publicity vehicle was to prove that acting was 'hard and serious work … and no one works at it more devotedly than Natalie Wood' then this image alone encapsulates all that she was endeavouring to become.

Wood entered into a delicate balancing act with her desires for both acting and stardom, seeing them as contradictory goals as she tried to capitalise on the success of *Rebel* but avoid biting the studio hand that had fed her all these years. 'You might say I'm going steady with acting, but I don't think being a movie star is a good enough reason for existing' (Tusher 1956, 64). Yet in the immediate aftermath, opportunities for good roles failed to appear and Wood needed the tricks of stardom to keep her in the public eye. Fan magazines vamped up the 'wild girl' image, alternately egging her on and then chastising her ('Teenage Tiger' 1957, 96). They reported on her romantic dalliances to prove that her commitment to acting was superficial. For a while after *Rebel*, she was seen in the arms of Scott Marlowe, a New York theatre actor trying to break into the movies. Journalists dismissed this as 'an intellectual phase', substituting her desire to be a serious New York actress with a New York boyfriend instead (Wilson 1956, AW20). Still another mocked her attraction to men who

are all fearfully, even depressingly, dedicated to acting, which they discuss at appalling length in the various Hollywood coffee shops and spaghetti joints they frequent. … Alas, none of them seem to have read much of the literature of this chosen profession (Robinson and Christian 1957, 48).

Other magazines rose to her defence. *Look* magazine retorted,

Fan magazines cluck with delighted dismay over her antics (*Is Natalie Riding for a Fall?*, *How Natalie Plays with Fire and Never Gets Burned*). But beneath her giddy exterior, she is an actress who is so ambitious that, according to a fellow-actor, 'if you tried to stop her, she'd cut you off at the knees' ('Teenage Tiger' 1957, 96).

In August, Warners arranged for a two-part special feature in *Photoplay*, entitled 'Don't Sell Natalie Short'. The article offered an apology of sorts for her wild antics by diverting attention from her sex life and back onto her acting. 'In many ways she *is* a rebel without a cause. She has not yet found out what satisfies and rewards her personally. In this respect she resembles millions of her contemporaries all over the world.' Wood, herself, provided a more complete picture of the dilemma facing a young Hollywood actress:

I don't know which side is the real side. I don't know which me is me. Sometimes I want to chuck my movie career and go and work on the New York stage. That might be more satisfying. And yet I like the idea of being Natalie Wood, the movie star. It's really fun. I don't know if I would enjoy being a nobody in a bit part on the New York stage (Gehman 1957a, 92).

Soon after Wood answered this question for herself by dumping all her Method-mopey boyfriends and eloping with the sleek Hollywood charmer Robert Wagner.

With Wagner, Wood suddenly became an ardent advocate for Hollywood glamour and mocked Method's angst:

'I for one am tired of hearing them complain about Hollywood,' she proclaimed. 'They don't really practice any method,' she said. 'I've gone to the Actor's Studio a few times to observe and have been impressed. I've also read all the books. And the methods boil down to just being honest and relating to the other person and most New York actors don't do it' (Hyams 1957, np).

Wood and Wagner held themselves up as the defenders of Hollywood glamour, mocking the 'nose-picking "Method" fringe group, who never got closer to the Actor's studio than Sunset Boulevard' (McDonald 1959, X7). Yet the nagging reality for Wood was that Warner Bros. was doing nothing to help her ascend to acting greatness, tossing her into B-level exploitation films about juvenile delinquency like the unintentionally hilarious *A Cry in the Night* and some Tab Hunter vehicles. Her one valiant effort, the prestige virgin melodrama *Marjorie Morningstar*, was undermined by a hamfisted director, Irving Rapper, whose conventional studio style generated none of the emotional intensity that Ray gave *Rebel Without a Cause*. Indeed, the film seems contemptuous of its own lead character (Sullivan 2010, 68). More promising was *Kings Go Forth*, a civil rights parable and pet project of mega-star Frank Sinatra, in which she plays a biracial woman 'passing' as white, caught in a torrid love triangle between two soldiers. While the film was only a moderate success rather than the blockbuster everyone hoped it would be, it gave her the opportunity to expand her sexual hysteric typecasting by applying it to the growing social debates about race and civil rights. While that racial ambiguity is discussed at great length in the following chapter, here the focus is on how Method directors extracted from Wood the performances she craved but retreated timidly from throughout her career.

Following her 'loan-out' to Fox to appear in *Kings Go Forth*, Wood provoked a stand-off with Warner Bros. The studio had wanted her to appear in Rapper's follow-up film, *The Miracle* (1959), about a young Spanish nun whose faith is tested by her lust for a passing soldier, and also offered her the lead in the classic pregnancy melodrama *A Summer Place* (1959). Wood refused them both (Finstad 2001, 247). The studio insisted she appear with its rising star Paul Newman in *The Young Philadelphians* (1959). When she failed to show up on the set, they suspended her for eight months, from July 1958 to March 1959. Yet well before the suspension was lifted, the studio was already planning a role for her that it knew she could not turn down. Warners optioned *Splendor in the Grass*, by celebrated playwright William Inge, signed director Elia Kazan, Nicholas Ray's mentor and Hollywood Method auteur, and let it be known through the trades that Wood was first choice for the lead role of Deanie (Connolly 1959, 2).

There are obvious similarities between Judy and Deanie. Both are sexually frustrated, romantically confused teenagers struggling to find a safe outlet for their unruly desires in a repressed society. The film begins in pre-Depression Kansas, as Deanie enjoys the attentions of high-school football star Bud, played by newcomer Warren Beatty, until his own desires get the better of him. Pained by his rejection and humiliated when he replaces her with the school's 'bad girl', Deanie has a nervous breakdown, throws herself at other boys and narrowly escapes rape, attempts to drown herself and is eventually incarcerated in a state asylum. There, she meets Johnny (Charles Robinson), a gentle young man with none of the animal magnetism of Bud. Meanwhile, Bud is tortured by lust until he finds comfort in the arms of Angie (Zohra Lampert), a young Italian immigrant girl who looks like a plainer version of Deanie. As Bud finally finds an outlet for his desires and Deanie learns to sublimate her own, their fortunes change. Bud's oil-baron father loses everything in the Stock Exchange collapse and commits suicide. Bud is reduced to a dirt farmer, now married to the perpetually pregnant Angie. Deanie's parents sold their stock before the crash in order to pay for her medical bills and achieve a comfortable middle-class living. Deanie marries Johnny, who becomes a doctor, and moves to Cincinnati. Yet after Bud and Deanie meet for one last goodbye, Bud kisses his wife passionately while Deanie drives off alone, reciting in her mind the lines from Wordsworth's 'Ode to Immortality' from which the film derived its title:

> Though nothing can bring back the hour
> Of splendour in the grass, of glory in the flower;
> We will grieve not, rather find
> Strength in what remains behind;

Casting Natalie Wood in *Splendor* capitalised on the lingering legacy of James Dean and *Rebel Without a Cause*, updated to embrace new levels of sexual liberation. The film is a frenzy of Freudian innuendo, elevating the razor-thin plot – should Bud and Deanie do it or not – to operatic levels. Yet those questions of teen lust and sexual authenticity were critical in mid-century America, so much so that Warner Bros. developed a 'controversy kit' for theatres, and rolled out an eighteen-city preview tour that had filmgoers answer a questionnaire which was then used in trade ads: 'Did you find anything censorable in the film?' 'Should Hollywood attempt themes such as this?' 'Would you want [children sixteen and over] to see the film?' Filmgoers overwhelmingly recorded their support of the film, sparking widespread anticipation of 'possibly the most controversial film to come along in any year' (*Splendor* pressbook). No longer an issue of delinquency and modern decay, sex between teenagers was now a private matter between two upstanding young adults mindful of their family obligations. The one constant was the hopeless ineptitude of the parents, unable to honestly confront their own desires and thus condemning their children to death-drive spirals of repression (Deanie) and hedonism (Bud).

Kazan obliquely referenced *Rebel* whenever asked about Wood's ability to bring one of his complex women characters to life, crediting himself with reviving her career.

I thought of Natalie then, because the leading female role again was that of a mixed-up teenager, but everybody warned me against her. They pointed out that she had made so many lousy pictures and that she was getting worse and worse (Davidson 1962, 32).

Yet despite his condescending assessment of her intellect: 'Natalie couldn't analyze *Finnegan's Wake*' (ibid., 34)), Kazan insisted that her acting instincts combined with ferocious ambition were enough to see her through the exhausting, demanding role.

Although she is not well educated, she has a good brain and she uses it. She is half woman, half child, and has a strong will. She is willing to do anything to be good. You see, Natalie is ambitious and therefore not contented with herself. This is one of the greatest assets an actress can have ('Beauty and Violence' 1961, 108).

Wood's performance under Kazan rivals only her work with Ray. The actor-driven intensity of Method directors Ray and Kazan gave her both the security and the confidence she needed to test her limits.

Kazan spent long hours with Wood, encouraging her to find her own way into the character and not to baulk at difficult moments. In a promotional interview for the film, she gushed, 'Before I did a scene, he'd ask me how I thought it should be done. No one had ever flattered me like that before, and this was the greatest director in the world to me' (Davidson 1962, 34). Similar to Ray, Kazan was a paternalistic director who favoured deep, personal relationships with his actors. Wood thrived under such tutelage, which was so unlike the business-like efficiency of studio-trained directors such as Rapper. In one interview, she openly contrasted her experience with Rapper to Kazan. During shooting of *Marjorie Morningstar*, she recalls being 'in tears the whole movie' because she was given nothing more than cues to reaction shots. Kazan, however, realised not only her potential but also her willingness to accept his guidance: 'She wanted a new career and I guess I gave her a new career' ('Movie Star into Actress' 1962, 55). Later, he said 'Natalie is still a little used to being made up like a doll and having some adult come along and tell her, "Get the hell over there and do this."' He happily obliged, and was credited for opening up 'a whole new phase of her career, a whole new phase of her intellectual approach to the making of pictures' (Bascombe 1963, 93).

The part of Deanie required a delicate touch in order to balance a glow of purity with increasing sexual deprivation. Wood's tiny frame and warbling voice conveyed the necessary emotional fragility and youthful innocence. Kazan stated,

I began to reason to myself that she was a natural, physically, for the part, and that if she worked hard and listened to me, I could probably free her from all the bad acting habits she had picked up in her many years in the business. She could cry on cue, for example, but only with her eyes. The rest of her face remained an impassive mask (ibid., 32).

Kazan spoke elsewhere about Wood's most striking feature: 'Her greatest asset is intensity … . This little white face with those black eyes peering out at you, sort of a hungry little girl – spiritually hungry, hungry for experience. She sort of clings to things with her eyes' ('Movie Star into Actress' 1962, 55).

Wood relies heavily throughout the film on flittering, fluttering eyes to register her slavish devotion to Bud, her sexual torment when he repeatedly rejects her and her quiet resignation to a passionless existence. Like Ray before him, Kazan stripped Wood of conventional movie-star glamour, fixing her hair and make-up to be as natural as Technicolor would allow. He wanted, both literally and figuratively, 'to put her up there naked and gasping' (ibid., 56). Wood's most famous scene in the film does just that, with her in the bathtub as her mother pushes her to the breaking point.

After Bud dumps her for Juanita (Jan Norris), the town's bad girl, Deanie collapses at school while reciting Wordsworth's 'Ode to Immortality'. At home, trying to escape her prying parents, she excuses herself from dinner to have a hot bath. Even in 1961, it would have been obvious to audiences that Deanie has masturbated in the bath and is now basking in the afterglow of orgasm. She sounds breathless as she tosses her head gently back and forth, her skin steaming and glowing from the hot water. As her mother intrudes and threatens to call Bud's parents, Deanie's reverie is violently disrupted. Her eyes, softly closed but still occupying the focal point of the screen suddenly explode open. As her voice rises with hysteria, Deanie covers her mouth and then bursts out of the tub. The camera swings behind her and pulls back, flirting with revealing as much nudity as possible. Her arms outstretched, she mocks her mother's obsession with her virtue, offering herself up as a sacrifice to American sexual hypocrisy. The camera wheels round to capture her iconic line in close-up, 'I'm a good little, good little, good little girl!' before retreating back behind her as she flees the scene. This play between naked body (from behind) and close-ups on a face contorted with rage and frustration highlight Wood's greatest physical strengths as an actor. Her petite frame or oversized eyes

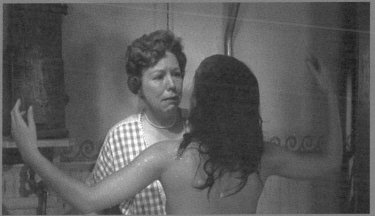

Splendor in the Grass (1961)

would not have been enough on their own to convey all the emotions necessary for this scene. It is in their jarring juxtaposition that all the anxieties of the era can be expressed.

As in *Rebel*, Wood was terrified of having to play this emotionally overwrought scene and sought refuge in technical tricks to bring on the tears. Unlike Ray, Kazan decided that the performance he was looking for couldn't come from desperation to please so he kept putting off filming while he coaxed Wood to take risks with her acting that she hadn't done in years. As she recalled:

Working with Kazan was like being reintroduced to that golden world that Nick Ray had given me a glimpse of. There was no director an actress could want to work for more in the fifties and sixties than Kazan. He was God. He taught me about being bold, not being afraid. I was actually very inhibited, but Kazan said, 'try things, risk it, don't worry about making a fool of yourself. Be bold. Be brave. Don't play it safe. What's the worst that can happen? Suppose you make a complete fool of yourself? We'll just do the scene again.' His teaching was a wonderful gift (Zimmerann 1963, 92).

Eventually Wood confessed to Kazan that her greatest anxiety was that he would demand that she cry on cue – something she had perfected while still a child but never without a sense of dread. He assured her, 'As long as you know what it is that you are feeling, and it's true for the character, it doesn't matter if you shed a tear or not. It's still going to be moving.' He also assured her that if she couldn't pull off the emotional intensity, he would shoot the whole scene from behind. Yet, Kazan, undergoing psychoanalysis himself at the time, decided he needed to conduct a little psychoanalytic treatment on his star to force an emotional catharsis. He asked Audrey Christie, who played Deanie's grasping, smothering mother, to start the scene with a line that Wood had confessed her mother would use on her. 'I went off the way I always used to and they shot it and that was it.' Wood plays the scene without tears but with wild-eyed ferocity. Kazan's

assistant director, Don Kranze, stated, 'From then on, it was easy. …
She broke open. She became a full-fledged – she was gonna hit that
role out of the park after that day' (Finstad 2001, 260).

Although the bathtub scene is by far the most famous, Kazan
always insisted that his favourite was the gentle, subdued finale as
Bud and Deanie say their last goodbyes to each other and to the
passions of youth (Young 1999, 264). It focuses mostly on Deanie,
who has sought out Bud to see if there's maybe one last chance for
them, but Bud has clearly moved on, with fond memories and few
regrets. After all the Freudian 'Sturm und Drang', and the outrage
directed at American sexual hypocrisy, Kazan's simple wish for the
closing of the film was to teach the audience to 'accept the cost of
disaster':

Deanie still has hope when she gets out of the hospital. She puts on a white
dress and goes out to visit Bud. She doesn't know what his situation is. She
finds him married. The marriage is not what you would call an ecstatically
happy one. But it's not an unhappy one either. He's sort of satisfied with it.
He doesn't want to give it up (ibid., 266).

As Bud's dilemma is resolved, the film's finale focuses on the final stage
of Deanie's emotional journey, a melancholy reflection on the high
costs of sexual desire for women. Whereas *Rebel* gave up on Judy as
soon as she gave in to Jim, *Splendor* seems more interested in
underscoring how women's sexuality must ultimately uphold what
Beth Bailey describes as 'a middle-class culture of respectability' (Bailey
1999, 76). Whether the argument was for chastity or sexual freedom,
the same civic appeals to exercise personal responsibility, citizenship
and maturity were used (ibid., 104). They speak to the general state of
confusion around sexual politics that made a film like *Splendor* a
surefire box-office hit – and Wood the obvious choice for its star.

Kazan wanted Wood because he recognised her potential in
Rebel Without a Cause. He also knew that he could acquire her dirt

cheap from Warners as it still had her locked in a penurious contract and, if she didn't settle with it soon, her career would be 'washed up' (Young 1999, 268). The studio knew it could capitalise on her reputation as a 'self-centred, self-indulgent, self-styled "free soul" [who has] stopped living it up and started to live' ('How Bob Changed Natalie' 1958, 69) to catapult her into more mature roles. In their promotional materials, they featured three images, all drawing attention to her expressive eyes. 'The Many Moods of Natalie Wood' included 'the wistful reveries of a restless teenager; the soul-ripping rage of a girl-woman struggling with her body's passions and heart's conscience; and the subtly emerging sensuality of a maturing young woman' (*Splendor* press book). It is the final scene that marks this last passage and delivers a message to young women to forswear passion for the good of the nation.

The scene introduces Angie as Bud's wife before Deanie realises he is married, then cuts to Bud who seems ambivalent about the prospect of seeing his old girlfriend again. Deanie, however, is teeming with excitement and when she runs to greet Bud she looks up at him adoringly just as in high school. The film relies on a series of close reaction shots as Wood widens and flutters her eyes, taking in Bud's lacklustre greeting, his ramshackle house, his slatternly wife and dirty child. Back outside, her eyes continue to dart anxiously while Bud talks about his life with Angie. She says – as a statement, not a question – 'You're happy Bud.' He agrees, 'I guess so,' and asks her the same but receives no answer except a non-definitive, 'Oh, I'm getting married next month.' Again, the camera closes in tight on her as she looks up beseechingly and says uncertainly, 'I think you might like him.'

When Deanie turns to go, Bud calls her back to say, 'I'm awfully glad to see you again.' Overwhelmed, she closes her eyes then, as she opens them, she gazes up at him, full of gratitude, before saying goodbye for the last time. Yet while Deanie appears to read this last gesture as evidence of his residual love for her, Bud returns to his house and passionately kisses Angie, who leads him seductively

Splendor in the Grass (1961) (BFI) (Warner
Bros./Photofest)

inside. He hesitates only briefly before following her. For Deanie, however, there will be no more passion. To her friend's question, 'Deanie, honey, do you think you still love him?' Deanie only smiles wistfully and stares straight ahead while the lines from Wordsworth's poem are recited in her mind. When she first delivered them, in her high-school classroom after Bud had humiliated her, it was in a shaky, emotionally choked voice that signalled the beginning of her nervous breakdown. Now, the words are spoken softly, barely above a whisper, but firmly and without any sense of regret or loss as her eyes are fixed in a steely gaze toward her passionless future. The film ends on a sweeping image of a lone rancher watching the car disappear in the dust as the music swells.

Arguably the most striking moment in the finale is the juxtaposition of Deanie and Angie as mirrors of each other's sexuality. Indeed Zohra Lampert, who plays the Italian immigrant Angie, was also of Russian descent and was evidently cast because of her likeness to Wood, minus the stunning beauty. Their colouring and hair are almost identical, as is the cut of their dresses, except Angie is frizzy and grimy from frying meat in the dirty kitchen. Her dress seems to be made from a sack and droops down over her breasts in a very unflattering way. She is pregnant and her posture suggests her body is already worn out by sex. Deanie, by contrast, is in an expensive white dress, gloves and pearls. Her purity, once a curse that drove her insane, is now a marker of respectability that has saved her from a lowly, sexually servile existence. Yet there is an ambivalence to this scene as the camera catches first Deanie then Angie looking down at themselves, registering embarrassment: Deanie by her airs of sophistication, Angie by her slovenliness.

The interplay between Angie and Deanie represents a much more ambiguous female sexuality than had been shown on screen in the past, one that allowed a degree of tempestuousness but stopped short of outright wantonness. Wood played this role better than anyone else in the period, even Elizabeth Taylor, to whom she was equently compared at this time. Whereas Taylor had ripened into undeniably full womanhood, aided and abetted by her romantic excesses, Wood 'didn't intimidate men, as Liz Taylor does, and other women could understand and like her because she wasn't that beautiful and they didn't feel challenged' (Benner 1988, 31). One Hollywood director, remarking on Wood's return to stardom, also pointed out,

Natalie is not as versatile an actress as Liz. I want to see Natalie play something else besides the poor, bewildered teenager. I admit no actress has ever matched Natalie on this, but playing the tormented teener is something with a limited life span in Hollywood. I want to see how she comes off as a woman (Crowley 1962, 95).

Unfortunately for this director, Wood did not take on this challenge. On Kazan's recommendation, she was next cast as the virginal, lust-filled teenager, Maria, in *West Side Story*. While it was also a critical and commercial hit, Wood veered away from the gritty New York school of film-making and settled comfortably back into the Hollywood star machine. She next starred in *Gypsy*, a brassy musical where she returned to a mawkish rendition of studio glamour that was nonetheless upstaged by Rosalind Russell as Mama Rose in every scene. In a 1963 *Life* magazine feature, 'Born to Be a Star' (182–8), Wood showcases her shrewd businesswoman tactics, surrounded by a fleet of grey-suited men hired to ensure that she 'earns a million dollars a year, along with something that means even more to her – the power and glory that stardom brings'. Although she insists that 'I'm not a star, I'm an actress,' the magazine retorts, 'But she still pulls all the trappings of stardom around her.' The feature contrasts sharply with the last time she had such prominence in this influential magazine. Here, she is not practising acting, but posing languorously on a stool, drenched in limelight while make-up and costume crew fuss around her. The magazine crows, 'Gowned in

'Born to Be a Star'. Photographed by Bill Ray for *Life* magazine
(1963) (Bill Ray/The LIFE Images Collection/Getty Images)

satin, bathed in spots, fussed over by attendants, Natalie glows with the glamor that a true star – and the movies themselves – never lost.'

Perhaps, just like before when Wood chose Hollywood over Method, the insecurities of acting at such a high intensity overwhelmed her. As Wood admitted much later in life,

I was working a helluva lot and my marriage was in trouble. I knew RJ [Wagner] and I loved each other, but I didn't like myself. I was insecure about my work, and I was suffering. I felt threatened by happiness, and I was doing everything to defeat even the possibility of it. Nothing seemed to be working out right. RJ and I split up and I went into psychoanalysis. Then my analyst died the following weekend. … I was shaking, and I knew that if I didn't hold on – just hold on – then I'd go over the edge (Pecheco 1979, 36).

Wood tried to refashion herself as a 'sophisticated movie queen' but few bought into it. 'She is soft and vulnerable, the kind of girl men hold tenderly, not passionately' said one critic. He continued by comparing her to Marilyn Monroe and insisted that 'there isn't that aura about her, and it's what she needs' (Zimmerann 1963, 95). Another critic agreed, this time comparing her to the other great sex symbol of the era. 'Natalie has everything going for her but her size … I know this may sound callous and technical, but … no girl with a thirty-two-inch bust, however well proportioned, will ever pose a threat to Liz Taylor' (Crowley 1962, 95). The press labelled her a 'Hollywood Throwback' and even Kazan threw his hands up in defeat,

… he watched Natalie make one of her typical grand entrances at a recent Hollywood premiere, wearing a kookie hat and heavy 1940s style makeup. He said, "Why does she have to look like that when she can look the way I have her on screen?" (Davidson 1962, 33).

As Zimmerann concluded, 'to be treated as a child is nice, but not in the pictures game' (1963, 95).

The biggest problem for Wood was that the Hollywood to which she was clinging was disappearing, along with a culture that had moved from debating sexual responsibility to demanding sexual freedom (Bailey 1999, 104). The adolescent social-problem films, once so controversial, now seemed as trite and artificial as the very conventions they seemed to repudiate. Newcomer film critic Pauline Kael was among the first to castigate the Method-lite histrionics and Technicolor melodrama that Hollywood called serious film-making, and she singled Natalie Wood out time and time again as the figurehead of this style. In her review of *West Side Story*, she managed to eviscerate Wood as both an actress and a star in one devastating sentence:

Like the new Princess telephone, so ingeniously constructed that it transcends its function and makes communication superfluous (it seems to be designed so that teen-agers can read advertising slogans at each other), Natalie Wood is the newly constructed love-goddess – so perfectly banal she destroys all thoughts of love (1962, 32).

With both the glamour-girl and serious-actress paths denied her, Wood floundered in roles that tried too hard at both. Meanwhile, Kazan and Ray faded away and with them Hollywood's first infatuation with Method. Thus, it is surprising that as late as 1966, with her career in a tailspin, Wood thought that her best chance at retrieving stature as a serious actress was to retread old Method territory with a cinematic adaptation of a minor one-act play by Tennessee Williams. The failure of *This Property Is Condemned* (1966) underscores all the reasons why *Rebel* and *Splendor* work – but only in their fleeting moment. Wood was the star of that moment, now relegated to Hollywood kitsch. *This Property Is Condemned* is a maudlin affair that some might say should have been better, given the pedigree of the cast and crew, but never really could have been, given the overworked and underdramatised plot of a woman undone by her sexual past. The 'soiled innocent' (Pecheco 1979, 36) had worked so well for Wood in the past, but she was now verging on thirty and had been dragged through the tabloid mud for so many torrid affairs that 'innocence' was no longer connected to her persona.

Starring Wood as a backwoods belle, newcomer Robert Redford as the man passing through town, directed by Sydney Pollack, with a screenplay by Francis Ford Coppola, based on the work of Tennessee Williams, this was to be, according to Wood, 'the closest I'll ever get to playing Blanche DuBois' (Lambert 2004, 228). As Alva Starr, the local beauty with a reputation, Wood delivers the naive coquette one more time, Redford plays her mildly abusive love interest, Owen Legate, with a wooden lack of intensity. Pollack's efforts to update the story material led to some strange directorial choices, including an upbeat score more in keeping with *My Fair Lady* than a story about a doomed sex worker, and sweeping crane shots just at the moment when the camera should be trained on Wood to allow her to reveal emotion. Indeed, the climactic scene, when Alva's mother tracks her down to New Orleans and tells Legate about her past, barely catches Wood on camera as she screams hysterically and runs out into the pouring rain. The camera keeps far back as she disappears into the night. The scene then cuts back to Alva's sister, who has been narrating the story in flashback, and says that Alva died of a lung infection as seems to be required of repentant prostitutes. When the camera does bother to focus on its lead star, it's at moments when Wood is supposed to portray innocence and pathos, which she does with an atrocious Southern accent and a perpetually cocked head tilting first one way then the other. Redford even recalls teasing her for that nervous tic, which seems to have replaced the widened eyes as her only way of expressing an inner emotional self (TCM Tribute).

While the film was supposed to mark a return 'to the "golden world" of Kazan and Ray' (Finstad 2001, 298), it was only as a stark reminder that cinema had moved on from the maudlin mid-century

This Property Is Condemned (1966)
(Paramount Pictures/Photofest)

vision of sexual mores. As Hollis Alpert noted, 'movies have been adapted so frequently from the works of Tennessee Williams that Hollywood is now able to whip up the familiar Southern mixture with very little help from the master himself'. The Blanche DuBois type had become caricature and thus, 'The tragic tale that unfolds is less suspenseful than expected, and very close to triteness as it heads remorselessly for the kind of climax that Williams himself surely would have avoided' (1966, 40). Even Williams agreed, as he had refused to cooperate with the making of the film and received only a roundabout credit of 'suggested by'. While Wood was shooting *This Property Is Condemned*, critics were already lining up to toss her into Hollywood's trash heap. Harvard Lampoon had awarded her 'worst actress for this year, next year, and 1968' ('Natalie Waves Thanks for Nothing' 1966, 44). Bosley Crowther lamented the dearth of adult roles and talented actresses to play them. Of Natalie Wood, he sneered, 'an aging teen-ager with all the presence of the girl next door' (1966, 93). Later in his review of the film, he lambasted Wood's performance in this 'soggy, sentimental story of po' little white trash' (1966, 24). Reviews of the film were more tepid than scathing, as if annoyed that they even had to bother.

Miss Wood plays the role as a girl strung taut and in herself theatrical ... . The trouble is that it takes a very strong, assured actress to play someone so false and nervous without calling the poise of her own performance into question, and Miss Wood seems always on the verge of missing a note (Adler 1966, 88).

Another mocked that Wood's character 'begins as a variant Laura Wingfield and ends as an apprentice Blanche DuBois' ('Boardinghouse Reach' 1966, 83). The formulaic portrayal of the 'wistful, sleazy Southern girl' (Alpert 1966, 40) did nothing to brighten Wood's fading star but merely provided fodder to critics that she was a middling actress relying on pretty mannerisms in increasingly tedious roles.

Shortly after *This Property Is Condemned* finished filming, Wood made several creative decisions that sealed her fate as 'one of the finest examples of [Hollywood's] manufactured products' (Hallowell 1968, 110). The first was turning down Warren Beatty's offer to co-star with him in *Bonnie and Clyde*. The second was to accept the lead role in a dreadful sex romp, *Penelope*. And then, for three years, nothing. Wood retreated completely from film-making for the first time since she was six years old. *Bonnie and Clyde* put the final nail in the coffin of Old Hollywood and the intense histrionics of mid-century Method were abandoned for a subtler form of acting than Wood could muster. Yet her performances in *Rebel Without a Cause* and *Splendor in the Grass* remain exemplars of American womanhood on the cusp of sexual revolution and suggest an imperfect, hesitant but nonetheless crucial moment in Hollywood's attempt to deal with radical social and sexual upheaval. While these are the two best known of that pre-revolutionary era, Wood also appeared in other far less successful films that showcased her at her limited best. The next chapter focuses on Wood's cinematic forays into the fraught terrain of American civil rights. Her roles in *Kings Go Forth* and *All the Fine Young Cannibals* offered new yet ultimately still too restrictive forms of sexual expression for women, turning Wood almost overnight from 'liberated ingénue' (Korba 1979, 11) to hackneyed cliché.

3 RACIAL AND SEXUAL AMBIGUITY

While Wood continued to be offered teen-rebel roles well past her own teen years, she sought out prestige film projects that could expand her acting range. The solution to her career stagnation, it seems, lay in her small role in *The Searchers*, in which she was cast as the pure white girl who passes into 'savage' sexuality as a wife of a Comanche chief and is then rescued and returned to colonial whiteness. Wood's exotic colouring contrasted with her petite, demure frame, making such radical transitions visually believable. In short, while the body supposed virginity and eternal girlishness, the eyes betrayed a sensuality and eroticism far beyond her years. Wood, the daughter of Russian immigrants, was cast in many ethnic and racial roles during the height of her fame, a typical pattern in Hollywood for 'white ethnic' women (Negra 2001, 2). During the violent era of civil rights and its immediate aftermath, Wood's 'passing' roles capitalised on her ethnic ambiguity to elevate her beyond adolescent-rebellion films and into the more hard-hitting terrain of racism. This chapter examines two of Wood's most intriguing 'passing' roles, *Kings Go Forth* and *All the Fine Young Cannibals*. These largely forgotten films hinge on tropes of racial mobility to signify the sexual and social status of Wood's characters. In the case of *Kings Go Forth*, Wood plays a classic 'tragic mulatta' caught in a love triangle between two white soldiers stationed in the south of France. In *All the Fine Young Cannibals*, Wood's Deep

South white trash character is sexually tormented by cool jazz and African American culture.

Kings Go Forth, a civil rights parable and pet project of mega-star Frank Sinatra, had all the earmarks of a prestige picture. Sinatra insisted that his studio, Fox, secure her as his love interest who keeps her biracial identity a dark secret. Wood was thrilled to get the role but furious with the terms of her loan to another studio, which netted Warner Bros. huge profits but kept her on regular salary (Lambert 2004, 134). Once filming for *Kings Go Forth* was completed, she exacerbated her tense relationship with the studio by turning down picture after picture until she was placed on probation on 15 July 1958, just four days before the film's premiere. She did not return to work until 24 February 1959, with a renegotiated contract that allowed her to make one non-Warner Bros. picture a year. The first film she selected was *All the Fine Young Cannibals*, an MGM melodrama which co-starred her new husband, Robert Wagner. Like *Kings Go Forth*, its love triangle was played against a backdrop of sentimentalised racial politics and a throbbing jazz soundtrack. Thus, both *Kings Go Forth* and *All the Fine Young Cannibals*, as the films which mark the beginning and end of her suspension from Warner Bros., also signal her transition from studio-controlled child star to independent actress. In these films, Wood experiments with an updated version of the sexual hysteric by incorporating racial politics. Wood plays women whose struggle with their desires will ultimately determine their racial identity in a deeply racist society.

Diane Negra articulates the difference between Euro-American 'white ethnicity' and African, Asian or Latin American identity. While racial otherness is more absolute, ethnic otherness contains a level of precariousness and instability (2001, 2). The ambiguous body of the ethnic American actress represents the promise of being elevated to whiteness through appropriate sexual and social behaviour. However, the melodramatic appeal of that body lies in its sublimated, libidinal desires that could send the body spiralling down into blackness (ibid., 3). Thus, an ethnic white actress could be more believable in a role where the drama was invested in resolving racial identity through sex. The confluence of darkness and Europeanness rendered her desirability less challenging – neither white enough to corrupt racial superiority nor black enough to disrupt racial purity (Wexman 1993, 140). What set Wood apart from other ethnic-immigrant stars like Anna Magnani and Sophia Loren was her excessively tiny frame. It belied the threat of erotic eruption and made her capitulation to middle-class American whiteness all the more credible. As David Savran notes, American postwar popular culture insisted that 'it was the task of men to control, rationalize and domesticate women and their dark sexuality, to ensure that "feminine" would forever remain a synonym for "submissive"' (1998, 175). Wood's unthreatening petiteness made her submission not only believable but inevitable.

Natalia Nikolaevna Zakharenko came of age during an era of racial, class and gender re-mapping across the country. She was 'Americanised' not once but twice, first when her parents legally changed her name to 'Natasha Gurdin' to sound less ethnic, and then when Hollywood erased all outward traces of Russianness by transforming her into 'Natalie Wood' at the age of six (Finstad 2001, 39). Nonetheless, her Hollywood handlers chose not to hide her ethnicity, but to exploit it as part of her special allure while still ensuring her status as a white American. From her first profile in *Life* magazine in 1945 and throughout her early career, magazines made reference to her Russian parents and her real name. However, they also took pains to emphasise her whiteness and occasionally exaggerate her parents' social status. One of the first feature articles on her labelled her a 'blonde moppet' – the studio dyed her hair – and promoted her father from stage carpenter to engineer ('New Movie Moppet' 1945, 87). As a teenager with dubious morality, Wood's hair became brown again and her new studio, Warner Bros., often cast her in ethnic 'passing' roles.

With Robert Wagner in *All the Fine Young Cannibals* (1960) (MGM/Photofest)

According to her biographer, Gavin Lambert, Wood was all too aware of her 'exotic' typecasting and worried about it narrowing her opportunities as a lead star but never to the point that she dyed her hair back (2004, 134). By the time she appeared in *Kings Go Forth*, she had already performed as the daughter stolen by Comanche in *The Searchers*, a Mexican half-breed in *The Burning Hills* (1956) and the titular Jewish princess in *Marjorie Morningstar*. Subsequently, many of her best-known roles were also either racial or ethnic 'passing' ones, most obviously as the Puerto Rican Maria in *West Side Story* and the Italian Angie in *Love with the Proper Stranger*. Thus, as Wood consciously sought to undergo a transformation from sexually wanton 'teenage tiger' to mature leading actress and dutiful wife, her own ethnic background became both an asset to her image makeover and a potential barrier to her reaching the highest levels of stardom.

What distinguishes her characters in *Kings Go Forth* and *All the Fine Young Cannibals* from her other 'passing' roles is that these films deal explicitly with African American racial identity and civil rights. While they approach the postwar problems of race and sex from opposite ends of a very rigid continuum, they employ similar techniques to register Wood's sexual status and to link it to her racial and class status as an unstable white body. Not only are her characters racially and sexually doubled, but so too is Wood herself. It is more than a coincidence that this critical juncture in her career comes at a time when she was attempting to rehabilitate her teen-rebel reputation and gain respect as an actress by touting her new-found sexual propriety. In this sense, her typecasting is not merely due to the fact that racism in Hollywood severely curtailed the possibility of casting non-white actresses in leading romantic roles. It also, to quote Pamela Wojcik, 'serves as a touchstone for ideologies of identity' through processes of doubled identification between star and role (2003, 229).

In *Kings Go Forth*, Wood plays Monique Blair, the beautiful and elegant daughter of a white mother and deceased black father, growing up in the south of France. Caught in a love triangle between the grim-but-good Sam Loggins (Frank Sinatra) and the jazz-playing charmer Britt Harris (Tony Curtis), both foot soldiers in World War II's 'Champagne Campaign', Monique's sexual awakening brings her suppressed racial identity violently to the surface. As Salome, a backwoods Texan, in *All the Fine Young Cannibals*, Wood is seduced by Robert Wagner after hearing him play jazz trumpet at a black brothel and she in turn seduces the wealthy 'Yale man' George Hamilton in order to secure a father for her illegitimate child. Both films conclude with Wood resigning herself to a compromised happiness by embracing a sexless mothering role that is coded as both white and upwardly mobile. This coding occurs through visual cues in the way her character is lit and dressed, and the environment in which she is surrounded. When erotically charged, she is in shadows, her body exaggerated and hyper-extended, juxtaposed with dramatic close-ups of her expressive eyes. When mastering her desires, she appears both small and rigid and is bathed in light, her eyes modestly downturned. The cues are not only visual, however. Both these films feature a cool West Coast jazz soundtrack with searing trumpet solos by her (white) love interests. Wini Breines comments on the centrality of jazz to postwar bohemia and the ability of the young, white middle class to escape the restrictions of bourgeois conformity in underground jazz clubs where interracial mingling was a sign of authenticity. Resolutely connected to African American culture, jazz also, problematically, represented the opportunity for white people to temporarily suspend their racial and class privilege and indulge in illicit pleasures without risk (2001, 141).

By the postwar era, 'race' was visualised on screen not merely (or even) through the physiognomy of the actor but through a vast array of cinematic devices to elaborate upon an identity that was more socio-psychical than biological or physical (Courtney 2004, 182). While ethnicity as a category may have been easier to assimilate and dissimulate, the barriers between races were made even more rigid – even as their construction became arbitrarily tied to social and sexual markers as much as skin colour. Mary Ann Doane argues that the representation of race in mid-century Hollywood cinema, in the absence of actual racialised actors, became based upon restrictive systems of gender and sexuality (1991, 246). Strictly upheld codes of heterosexuality, patriarchy and gender difference determined the race of an otherwise troubled body on screen; which in turn determined that body's access to the middle class, characterised by a commitment to traditional gender roles within a nuclear family. Richard Dyer elucidates this point by arguing that it is heterosexuality that binds race and gender together, as it defines the latter and reproduces the former. Desire furnishes the conditions for the continuation of the races, but desire itself is coded as darkness and represents a betrayal of whiteness even as it is its salvation (1997, 28). What brings *Kings Go Forth* and *All the Fine Young Cannibals* together here is that they represent competing yet complementary ends of this racial-character debate and its corresponding concerns with sexuality: a white woman revealed to have some deep-set blackness residing within her, stirred up by sexual desires, only to be resublimated in order to ascend to middle-class maternalism within the hierarchies of whiteness.

Sinatra was a staunch advocate of civil rights, appearing in anti-racism propaganda films, writing essays on racism in popular magazines and never hesitating to remind others of his own background as a working-class Italian American. He had high hopes that *Kings Go Forth* could situate racism as a distinctly American problem, one that prevented the nation from achieving its true goals of democracy, plurality and freedom (McNally 2008, 84). Thus, the characters all come from the Northeastern seaboard, instead of having the racist cad who seduces and abandons Monique hail from Mississippi as was the case in the novel. As part of the promotion for the film, Sinatra wrote an essay for *Ebony* magazine in which he claimed,

> A friend to me has no race, no class, and belongs to no minority. My friendships were formed out of affection, mutual respect, and a feeling of having something strong in common. These are eternal values that cannot be racially classified. This is the way I look at race (ibid.).

Thus, the film sought to argue against racial difference in favour of an immutable identity of Americanness, played out against a backdrop of unquestioned gender roles and middle-class aspirations.

Since Wood, as Curtis noted drily, 'didn't look remotely Negro' (ibid.), Monique's racial ambiguity is signalled through a series of visual clues. Sam first spots her as he wanders aimlessly along the seawall, soldiers carousing with local women in the background. By contrast, Monique sits apart with a young child and is teaching him to count. The camera moves to her face, which is framed in black: her turtleneck, her sleek hair, her long lashes. But the skin is pale, the features delicate and her smile demure. In the background, the dark waters of the Mediterranean contrast with the bright white yachts bobbing in the waves. The racial ambiguity is underscored by Sam's ambivalent voiceover narrative as the camera lingers over Monique's face: 'I try now to remember what I thought in the first moment. She was beautiful, I guess.'

Despite her initial resistance, and with her mother's permission, Sam begins to court her, leaving his army camp to visit them often in their refined French villa. He tells her of his life back home in Harlem, where his boss was about to make him partner before the war intervened. His story is the classic American Dream of the working-class child of immigrants ascending into the middle class once his service to his adopted country is completed. Monique, the educated and genteel daughter of ex-pat Americans, appears to be the perfect helpmate on this journey upward. One night, in her impeccably manicured garden, he steals a quick kiss on her shoulder. As she turns to gently protest, the camera hints again at the secret about to be revealed. Sinatra is bathed in light while Wood's face is shrouded in darkness. She rebuffs him coldly, willing to let him walk away. It is her mother, a regal and still-beautiful woman, who beckons him back into their classically French drawing room so that he may discover the truth about Monique: her deceased father was black.

Despite the heavily ornate room, no picture of Monique's father is on display. Instead Mrs Blair (Leora Dana) hands Sam a portfolio so he can see the evidence for himself. Importantly, the audience never sees Monique's father, so he remains invisible and enigmatic. It is, therefore, from her mother that Monique's racial identity is inherited. Thus, Monique is able to 'pass' as white but it is a polluted whiteness that requires the erasure of the father and a resolve not to reproduce her mother's transgression (Anderson 1997, 46). The film enforces this image of Monique as white by framing her disclosure within a highly refined, classically European interior, 'the perceptual plenitude of cinematic sound and image' (Courtney 2004, 174). As she enters from the pitch black of the garden into this cultured space, Monique re-secures her whiteness. The black inside her is in fact external to her cultivated environment. Even so, there is a dark shadow on the wall, a lurking threat that her blackness may free itself from her body at any moment.

Having resolved not to let his prejudice keep him from love, Sam returns and takes Monique out to a smoky little jazz club called Le Chat Noir. It is there that she meets Britt, a charming rogue from Sam's unit, when he is called to join the band. He has already been introduced as Sam's nemesis. Whereas Sam comes from the hard-knock streets of New York's racially mixed Harlem district, Britt is the suave and pampered son of a mill owner raised in a bucolic small town in upper New York State. Yet here is Britt indulging in and even blending into a culture that should more truly belong to Sam. Britt begins a virtuoso trumpet solo, his hips thrusting provocatively to the beat as he stretches his horn upward, and a transformation comes over Monique. In a series of cut-away close-ups, Monique's rising

Kings Go Forth (1958)

attraction is demonstrated by her eyelids fluttering distractedly and
her body unconsciously swaying to the music. Interestingly, each
time the camera moves to a close-up of her, there is also a prominent
shadow of another woman, dragging heavily on a cigarette, on the
wall directly behind her. At no time during the scene is the owner of
that shadow present, it seems to both belong to and to not be a part
of Monique. Britt joins them and physically manoeuvres Sam out of
the threesome, talking jazz with an increasingly enthralled Monique.
In his controversial 1957 essay, 'The White Negro', Norman Mailer
argues that 'jazz is orgasm, it is the music of orgasm, good orgasm
and bad, and so it spoke across a nation' (1959, 341). Britt's phallic
performance, Monique's sexual stirrings and her repressed African
American roots collide in a metonymic catharsis that irrevocably

Kings Go Forth

links her sexuality to her racial identity. As one reviewer of the film remarked sarcastically, 'even Monique's French upbringing cannot assuage the jazz-tremors of her American Negro heritage' (Johnson 1959, 41).

Now it is another American soldier courting her, but the circumstances, and her racial association, are transformed by the fact that she reciprocates the erotic desire. As Sam's unease increases, Britt and Monique stroll out to the boardwalk. There are parallels to her first encounters with Sam. She is once more standing against the ocean, now a bottomless pit of rippling blackness. And she is wearing the same dress she wore in the garden the night she confessed her secret. They share a long, passionate embrace, the camera pulled in tight, Monique's face shrouded in darkness as Britt smothers her with kisses. The camera then pulls back as Monique steps hesitantly away from Britt, that once demure dress now fluttering sultrily from behind, exposing a silhouette of her body as a low jazz saxophone plays. Sander Gilman discusses how the display of exaggerated buttocks in both western art and medicine is intended to indicate 'hidden sexual signs, both physical and temperamental, of the black female' (1985, 219). Up until now, Monique's clothing has been austerely tailored and modest. Yet, the same outfit she wore when she confessed her secret blackness to Sam, a dress that appeared the epitome of feminine daintiness in the drawing room, is now a swirling sheath that seems to be breaking free of her tiny body.

At Sam's insistence, Britt agrees to marry Monique, but claims that the army is moving slowly on the paperwork. Eventually Sam discovers Britt is lying and forces a confrontation in the same drawing room where Monique first confessed her secret to Sam. Britt admits that he was only toying with Monique because he'd never had a black woman before. Allison Graham argues that this scene reveals a form of white 'passing': Britt, despite his racial and class privileges, is nothing more than 'scum', as Mrs Blair calls him. Nonetheless, his betrayal forces Monique to expose herself as hysterically black (2001, 34). The camera closes in tight as she screams violently then flees out the same garden doors from which she had passed from blackness into whiteness for Sam, only this time it is back into blackness. Eventually Sam finds her, half-drowned on the docks. Thus, Monique fulfils the narrative requirements of the tragic mulatta in the sense that she kills all sexual desire and therefore the blackness in her (Anderson 1997, 53). However (and in contrast to the book in which she does die), Monique successfully negotiates her way back to whiteness by dedicating her life to celibate, maternal service as a schoolteacher to war orphans. The conclusion caused one reviewer to mock 'the moviemakers' striking contribution to contemporary sociology – a general solution for the social and emotional problems of the mulatto. The solution: give up sex' ('Kings Go Forth' 1958, 82).

Thus, within the logic of postwar Hollywood cinema, the erotic disposition of a woman can transform her racial identity. An actress like Wood, therefore, possessed all the requisite contradictions to elucidate the anxieties of race and sex in postwar American culture. As an ethnic-American actress less appreciated at this time for her talent than for her sexual escapades, her racial mobility is all the more believable. This is further borne out in the next major role Wood played in this transitional phase of her career, that of poor white-trash Sarah who renames herself Salome and induces a sexual rivalry between her melancholy jazz lover and rich but emasculated husband. *All the Fine Young Cannibals* is shot with moody blue and grey exteriors and excessively stylised interiors to signify either Old World, feminised wealth or modern, Playboy-chic urbanity. The film might have aspired to mimic the heightened melodramatic style of Douglas Sirk, but it lacked the requisite irony or psychoanalytic complexity to pull this off. Billed as a 'drama of today's youth', the film promised 'They smash all rules ... they know no limit ... in the love-hungry world of the sophisticated young moderns!' The hope for Wagner and Wood was that this film would catapult them back to the top of the Hollywood heap, as lead actors in the new youth-driven but high-minded cinema culture that had begun with the already iconic *Rebel Without a Cause*. Underscoring these aspirations of authenticity and rebellion were the racial subplot and the jazz-filled narrative that would bring the lovers together, tear them apart and ultimately be set aside for, as the script synopsis stated, 'a new maturity, a soberer sense of tolerance and the fallibility of human understanding' (*All the Fine Young Cannibals* PCA Files 22 May 1959).

Following the death of his father, the local preacher, Chad (Robert Wagner) takes Salome (Natalie Wood) to a saloon/brothel run by a motherly black woman named Rose (Louise Beavers). She insists he plays the trumpet to ease his grief and introduces him to the crowd, 'all of Chad's tunes are original, heart-breaking and composed on the spot'. And so he moves through the saloon, playing an improvisational string of melancholy melodies, as the black patrons stand respectfully, slowly moving in time with the music. Just behind Salome's left shoulder is a young black woman. She is only visible in this shot because of a continuity error. Previously, Salome was positioned to the right and in front of the band, and the woman was seated on a man's lap just to the left of her. When the camera moves to this medium close-up, Salome apparently has stepped forward and turned so that this woman – now sitting on a chair with another woman's hand resting on her shoulder – can share the frame with her. When the camera returns to Chad, Salome is back in front of the band and the woman is blocked from view by the back of Chad. The camera cuts back again to the shot of Salome and once again that same woman sits and stares immovably into the camera, sharing the frame with Salome. Where Salome is lit high and bright and is wearing a pale pink dress, the woman in the background is lit low and dark and dressed in blue. Like the dark shadow looming over Monique in the jazz club, these two flickering cutaways present a white female subjectivity divided between a bourgeois order of domesticated heterosexuality and a darker world of 'wild sexuality and violence' (Rowe and Lindsey 2003, 174). Unlike Monique, whose blackness is betrayed by her wide, fluttering eyes, Salome casts her eyes downward and averts her gaze so that no one should see her sexual arousal while her black doppelganger stares immovably ahead.

Having been sexually awakened by jazz music, surrounded by black women of dubious moral character, Salome races into the night with Chad. Soon after, she realises she is pregnant and convinces Chad to let her run away on her own. On the train, she meets and seduces a young man who she first encountered that night in the brothel, a wealthy young Yale student from Dallas named Tony (George Hamilton). As the train hurtles through the night, enlisting one of Hollywood's most trusted clichés to connote sex, the scene cuts violently back to a silhouette of Chad waking from a nightmare yelling, 'Dark!! Dark!! I got to have some kind of light!' He takes refuge back at the saloon where he meets Ruby (Pearl Bailey), Rose's sister. Chad recognises her as a famous singer, but she has now returned to Deep Elm from New York to drink herself to death. The film does not definitively reveal whether they become lovers. Although Wagner claims in his biography that love scenes between him and Bailey were cut, there appears to be scant evidence of this in correspondence between the studio and representatives for the Production Code Office (Wagner 2008, 175). Regardless, the next sequence shows Tony and Salome eloping while Chad blows his trumpet triumphantly in Ruby's bedroom as they decide to run off together to New York to launch Chad's musical career.

Salome's stress of keeping up her masquerade after the birth of her son, Peter, is exacerbated by the introduction of Tony's spoiled sister, Catherine (Susan Koehner). One night, while lying in a sexless marital bed, the white ruffled curtains on her window flutter as a mournful jazz trumpet wafts through the room. Although the focus is on Salome, she is deep in shadow, while Tony, who is merely background to this scene, is bathed in soft light. She arises and drifts downstairs, following the music, her tight white negligé flowing seductively around her blacked-out body. Just as with Monique, her petite frame is exaggerated into an hourglass shape with additional emphasis given to her hips and buttocks. Once she enters the living room she discovers Catherine with a young man, listening to a record by the New York sensation, Chad Bixby. After Salome tricks Tony into taking them to see Chad perform, the film enters into a love quadrangle involving Salome and Tony, Chad and Catherine – who elope soon after. The conflicts between them are not resolved until Ruby dies and Chad and Salome discover somewhat unconvincingly that they no longer love each other but want to remain with their respective (and respectably wealthy) spouses.

All the Fine Young Cannibals (1960)

Rather than the tragic mulatta, here Wood's character resembles more the Jezebel, the sexually uncontrollable black woman whom Anderson suggests represents a dangerous temptation to white men and therefore to the patriarchal white family upon which American idealism is grounded (1997, 88). Indeed, the name she chooses for herself, Salome, is that of the Biblical figure who seduced Herod into executing John the Baptist in order to save her mother from accusations of adultery. Both Jezebel and Salome are bound by sins of sexual transgression. Thus, even though Wood's Salome is not black even by part, her ability to ensnare men into falling hopelessly in love with her, and her inability to control her own erotic desires make her the embodiment of a dangerously uncontrolled female sexuality that is coded as black. Graham refers to this type of character as a 'cultural mulatto', her racial ambiguity defined by her low-class status and unchecked sexual desires while buttressed by a cinematic environment of black culture, in this case jazz (2001, 30).

Salome's black self continues to exert its presence on screen, both through the visual envelope that surrounds her but also, more tellingly, through the character of Ruby. As Chad's true erotic and artistic passion, she is 'one body too much' (Doane, 1991, 235), the racial force that disrupts an otherwise too-neat sexual quadrangle. Ruby fulfils the role of the black woman undone by sex when she decides to drink herself to death after her lover, the trumpet player in her band, leaves her for another woman. There are some subtle hints that this lover may have been white in the way she relates to Chad and seeks to make him over, even giving him her lover's coat. She tells Chad,

I loved that man who played horn for me, I loved him deep and wide. I gave him everything I ever had. I told you that. I gave him money. He spent it on another gal. Respectable and educated. He married her. Almost two months ago. At just the exact time that Ruby Jones happened to die.

Having turned her back on her successful singing career in New York, Ruby is lured back by Chad to help establish him as a jazz sensation. At his first headlining show, she sings one more time before collapsing and proclaiming that it is now time for her to die. She retreats to the bedroom of their opulent, bordello-like apartment while Chad continues his meteoric rise to the top of New York's jazz scene, and remains there as his tragic muse, offering legitimacy and authenticity not only to Chad's jazz aspirations but also to his hipster affectations.

Once Ruby is dead, Chad and Salome are somehow magically freed from their jazz-induced passion for each other and can assume the proper roles in their sanctioned marriages. Krin Gabbard argues that the standard jazz narrative of Hollywood implies that jazz is somehow incompatible with romance, and that all jazz men – black and white – must ultimately reject that bohemian world in order to take back their place as domesticated patriarch (Gabbard 1996, 157). In that sense, race and sex are once again entwined with class to mutually reinforce whiteness, heteronormativity and middle-class identity as the only indications of maturity that matter. After Salome confesses to Tony that Chad is the real father of their child, she returns as the prodigal daughter to her father's home and resumes her life of domestic drudgery. When Tony arrives on the porch, to the delighted squeal of his son, Salome remains silent in the doorway, framed by the domestic responsibilities she has finally resolved to embrace. Her natural, care-worn face is the last image of the film as she whispers softly, 'My name is Sarah.' This other biblical figure is, of course, one of the most respected matriarchs of the Old Testament, wife of Abraham, mother of Isaac and the only woman to whom God spoke directly. Wood plays this scene drawing once again on the most expressive of her features, her eyes. They dart up and down and flutter modestly before looking serenely but without longing toward her reunited family.

By spurning eroticism and even once-removing the sex act that comes with reproduction (since Tony is not the father), Sarah is able to regain her place within 'innocent white womanhood' (hooks 2015, 159). By choosing Tony over Chad, she removes the taint of blackness that was destroying her and everyone around her. This is confirmed by that final image which presents Sarah in what Gwendolin Foster calls full whiteface: 'a space of representation that demands class-passing, class othering, giving up ethnic identity to become white, and insists that the human race, especially in America, is white' (2003, 51). That this whiteness is achieved by acquiescing to the traditional gender roles prescribed by heterosexual bourgeois domesticity only further entrenches the notion that, in postwar Hollywood at least, racial identity could be secured through sexual identity. Not only did Wood achieve that masquerade in these two films, but also in her new life as a happily married wife and domesticated hostess, firmly committed to upholding the old Hollywood traditions against the tides of social change.

In a rare interview just after her suspension from Warner Bros., Wagner and Wood declared themselves the last of the old-school movie stars in Hollywood. 'Some guy made a crack that Natalie and I are trying to act like movie stars. I told him it was about time that somebody in this town did.' Wagner told the *New York Times* before that he and Wood ridiculed angst-based acting. 'The idea of Hollywood neurotics is also nonsense. You have problems anywhere. At least in Hollywood you get well paid for them,' Natalie added (McDonald 1959, X7). This new attitude was a far cry from the teenager who would spring into improvisational performances on street corners with her *Rebel* friends Dennis Hopper and Nick Adams, or watched *A Streetcar Named Desire* over and over to catch the nuances in Vivien Leigh's performance. Wood's shift in attitude toward acting was echoed in her deference to Wagner as the titular head of their household – despite the fact that she was the bigger star, even when on suspension. 'As far as I'm concerned R. J. will always be, without any possibility of any argument, the head of the family. That's a husband's traditional role, and to controvert it would only be an invitation to trouble' ('Natalie Wood on Marriage' 18 April 1959).

Wood likened her role in *All the Fine Young Cannibals* to her new-found maturity as a happily married woman. As she said with all the wisdom of a twenty-one-year-old,

[Cannibals] is very involved with problems of young people who don't know how to love wisely and who make mistakes and destroy their lives. It's completely realistic … with no fairytale ending. It shows that people have to be mature and be honest with each other to find lasting happiness (Mann 1960, 56).

Maturity in this case meant learning how to cook, clean and play hostess. Her husband approved wholeheartedly, 'I believe that the woman is the most important facet in married life. She sets the pattern. She makes the home and social life. And in our particular case, she is a full business partner' (Parsons 1960, 58). Wood's persistent disavowal of her wild past and the culture associated with it – Method acting, Freudian psychology and adventures in bohemia – coupled with a picture-perfect marriage to a strait-laced ambassador of old-fashioned values, sought to exemplify exactly what her acting roles of this period appeared to claim: only by being demure and capitulating to middle-class domesticity could a woman properly achieve an authentic sense of self. The roles she chose at this crucial juncture in her career link sexual propriety and middle-class conformity to whiteness. Wood was remarkably well suited for such roles because of her ethnically marked body and her sexually marked past.

The star persona of Natalie Wood, a character as constructed as the roles she played, embodied national cultural anxieties over race and sex – and their resolution. Thus, her selection of these two roles – a good black woman trying to be white, and a bad white woman temporarily giving into her blackness – reflects not only the spatial and temporal specificities of postwar racial politics but also demonstrates their relationship to gender and sexuality and the way in which all these identity traces were performed both on and off the screen to create the American actress known as Natalie Wood. In effect, then, Hollywood needed a star like Natalie Wood to help navigate through this postwar project of national identity-building. Despite the failures of both these films, and her contentious attitude toward her studio bosses, Hollywood could not give up on Natalie Wood quite yet. With her next three films, Wood was catapulted to the height of the stardom she had been working toward since the age of four. She made it to the top by playing sexually and racially marked characters that struck a tenuous balance between the psychoanalysis-infused artistry of the New Hollywood and the glamorous affectations of the Old. This delicate combination was fast losing its charm. Thus, this chapter concludes by considering her most successful role in both 'passing' and hysteria, Maria in *West Side Story*.

By the time Wood was cast in *West Side Story*, her marriage to Wagner was crumbling and she was loath to do yet another ingénue role, much less an 'exotic' one. Her co-stars were equally loath to have her in the lead, seeing her as nothing more than a box-office attraction without the skill or talent to play Maria, the sweet Puerto

Rican immigrant who falls for her brother's arch rival. She kept herself isolated on set, was rude to her romantic lead, Richard Beymer (Tony), and quickly lost the respect of the rest of the cast. Rita Moreno, who played her best friend, Anita, recalls, 'Maybe when you feel you're not up to the job, you sort of give up on it, you go through the motions' (Finstad 2001, 269). As a result, the 'passing' of Natalie Wood as Puerto Rican is nothing less than disastrous, between her ludicrous accent and her own make-up and wardrobe team that was more interested in making her look like a young Hollywood star than a newly arrived immigrant. There are really two films happening on screen, the first with its exuberant and expansive dance sequences that make the most of CinemaScope technology, and the tightly shot romantic scenes between two woefully miscast and chemistry-less actors on cloistered backlots. Wood fell back on the reliable tropes of star acting: wide eyes set off by a gently cocked head to convey an arch naivety, and a tightly controlled body that collapses into hysteria only to wind back up into itself. Yet, despite all these problems, the film works and Wood received high praise from most critics. In the *New York Times,* Bosley Crowther singled her out for her strong performance (1961, X1) and the *Saturday Review* said 'Natalie Wood is radiant as Maria in love, deeply moving in her tragic moments' (Knight 1961, 40). A notable exception was Pauline Kael, whose disdain for Wood never let up for the rest of both their careers.

The film is a contemporary, urban retelling of *Romeo and Juliet,* with Wood as the younger sister of the Puerto Rican gang leader Bernardo (George Chakiris), and Beymer as the now-reformed rival gang leader Tony. Racial and immigrant politics collide on the streets of New York as the previous generation of Euro-American ethnic immigrant working-class kids clash with the new Latin American immigrants. Negra's distinctions between ethnicity and race are important here, especially as Puerto Ricans occupied a much more ambivalent space somewhere between ethnic and racial identity.

Loveman and Muniz argue that throughout the first half of the twentieth century, mutually reinforcing patterns of 'boundary crossing' by individuals who changed their racial self-identification and 'boundary shifting', as the census definitions of what constituted 'white/mulatto/black' (the categories provided in the official census) changed, rapidly transformed the population so that by 1950, 80 per cent of Puerto Ricans identified as white (2007, 915). Yet Frances Negrón-Muntaner notes that Puerto Rican Americans still strongly associate their representation in *West Side Story* with the racism they experience (2000, 84). The casting of Wood, and the way that she is separated out from the ensemble both on screen and throughout the production, exacerbates this confusion over racial identity. Her own boundary crossing is signified by the romantic storyline, contrasting sharply with the tempestuous and hot-tempered Anita, who is Bernardo's girlfriend and Maria's confidante – and played by a Puerto Rican actress. Thus, once again, it is sexual propriety that elevates Maria above Anita: her lust is tempered by fantasies of white weddings and an escape to an imagined 'somewhere' in America. That sexual difference is doubled back on itself by the racial identity of the actresses – Wood an ethnic white Euro-American and Moreno a Latina.

According to Robert Wise, Wood was 'perfect physically' for the role of Maria, noting in particular her dark eyes and small stature and downplaying her racial ambiguity by complimenting her adaptability to different roles and insisting that she and Moreno were working closely together on her accent ('Beauty and Violence' 1961, 106). In an era of sideways casting for race, Wood was commended for having 'the right dark glow as the Latin heroine', rather than criticised for trying to pass as Puerto Rican. In the same review, Moreno was praised as a 'nubile Nurse' who was 'strikingly slummy' ('Sweetness & Blight' 1961, 94). The story of Wood's casting goes that it was Kazan, still intent on making Wood his latest Galatea-like triumph, who convinced Jerome Robbins to cast

With Rita Moreno in *West Side Story* (1961)
(United Artists/Photofest)

her. He said, 'How unknown can you get after being buried in
pictures like *All the Fine Young Cannibals*?' He showed Robbins
early footage from *Splendor in the Grass* to prove that Wood could
handily pull off the tormented teenager and 'pass' as Puerto Rican
enough to meet Hollywood's racist casting criteria (Davidson 1962,
32). As Negrón-Muntaner argues, the fact that it was well known
that Wood was Russian American, not Latina, made it possible for
'white audiences to enjoy the interracial seduction without its
consequences'. The result is, 'a drag ball of sorts, where white
(male) America can inhabit the dark and dangerous skins of Puerto
Ricans, and desire Natalie Wood safely (protected by her
whiteness) while indulging in Rita Moreno from Bernardo's
masquerade' (2000, 92).

As Hollywood transitioned away from the studio system and actors cultivated outsider, independent status as artists, Wood doubled down on the glamorous star acting that catapulted her to fame. She completed her trifecta of Hollywood stardom with the big, brassy musical *Gypsy*, in which she plays burlesque queen Gypsy Rose Lee against Rosalind Russell's scene-chewing performance of stage mother extraordinaire Mama Rose. Immediately after, Wood's career once again sputtered to a halt. She alternated between over-the-top sex farces like *Sex and the Single Girl* (1964) or *The Great Race* (1965) and a retreading of sexual rebellion in *Love with the Proper Stranger*, *Inside Daisy Clover* and *This Property Is Condemned*. They all met with tepid reviews and increasing disinterest in her limited stable of acting tricks (Whitman 1967, 35). By the mid-sixties, the old rules of studio stardom no longer prevailed. In a culture looking for grainy authenticity, not Technicolor histrionics, Wood was openly mocked in the press as a parodic relic of Old Hollywood. She stuck doggedly to the traditional family-oriented Freudian psychoanalysis that kept her on the couch since her break-up with Robert Wagner in 1962. A string of disappointing relationships with Hollywood bad boys (Warren Beatty, Henry Jaglom) and old guard alike (Frank Sinatra) had turned her into an object of pity in fan magazines (Waterbury 1966, 76). Suddenly, after two decades of struggling to stay in the public eye, Wood retreated from view for three years, returning briefly at the end of the sixties to cement her place as the last of the old-style Hollywood stars.

4 A SEXUAL LIBERTINE IN THE SUBURBS

After five failed films in a row, from 1964–6, Wood moved to London to live with her fiancé, British producer Richard Gregson. It was the longest hiatus from the film set in her career and the only time, other than during her suspension by Warner Bros., in which she did not appear in at least one film or television series per year since she was eight years old. Wood clarified that her decision to withdraw from her career was so she could focus on herself as a person rather than as a star. 'I didn't know who the hell I was. … I was whoever *they* wanted me to be' (Pecheco 1979, 38). Through psychoanalysis she came to a rather classical Freudian conclusion: '"Natalie Wood" may have craved stardom, but *she* always desired a family' (Finstad 2001, 309). After this self-imposed exile, Wood returned to Hollywood to star in the iconic sex comedy *Bob & Carol & Ted & Alice*, which put her back on the top of the Hollywood heap. However, the realisation that she was pregnant with her first child halted her film ambitions as she placed her focus on her new marriage and baby Natasha, born in 1970. When the marriage failed after just two years, the celebrity gossip world was stunned to learn that she was back with Robert Wagner. They remarried in 1972 and had a daughter, Courtney, two years later. After this spurt of media attention, Wood again withdrew from the limelight, appearing sporadically in television movies and specials for the next ten years. Her one film in the decade following *Bob & Carol & Ted & Alice* was *Peeper* (1976), a flat-footed romp co-starring Michael Caine, made just before Courtney's birth. After that, her rare appearances in the media were almost exclusively in family and home magazines, where she and Wagner extolled the virtues of stay-at-home motherhood, marital fidelity and tasteful decorating.

In 1979, ten years after her last major success, Wood attempted another comeback. Her first foray back onto the film set was the big-budget film *Meteor* (1979), co-starring Sean Connery. It was part of the disaster film trend of the seventies, which tended to feature ageing Hollywood stars who had been absent from the screen for some time. Unfortunately, *Meteor* came well at the end of the trend, which began properly in 1970 with the release of *Airport* and peaked in 1974 with such films as *Earthquake* and *The Towering Inferno* (which featured Robert Wagner). A major disappointment, the film did nothing to re-ignite her career, representing little more than an exercise in nostalgia. She then begged her old friend Robert Redford to cast her in the role of the brittle, emotionally barren mother in the film *Ordinary People* (1980). Despite Redford's sense of indebtedness to her for launching his career with *Inside Daisy Clover*, he ruefully refused. Wood never spoke to him again (Finstad 2001, 370).

Instead of *Ordinary People*, Wood signed on to play the wife/mother lead in another film about marital and family breakdowns. *The Last Married Couple in America*, co-starring George Segal, is a sitcom-level romantic comedy about a happily married couple in Los Angeles who react to the pressure of the times by exploring alternative sexual relationships. Released in February 1980, *The Last Married Couple in America* would be her final completed film. Wood died by drowning on 29 November 1981. Taken together as the beginning and end of the last phase of her career, *Bob & Carol & Ted & Alice* and *The Last Married Couple in America* offer a portrait of Wood as the ingénue in midlife crisis. With these films and with her own decision to temporarily pause her career to focus on marriage and motherhood, Wood reflects the breakdown of American postwar society from a particularly distinct vantage point. It was her generation – caught between the 'Greatest Generation' of World War II veterans and the self-declared revolutionary baby boomers – that experimented the most with sex education, desegregation, Freudianism, personalism, birth control, consciousness raising and a host of other forms of liberal social engineering (Pells 2010). The general tone of her sporadic film and media appearances in the seventies suggests that Wood was determined not only to secure her legacy but also to publicly legitimate all her choices to date and insist on their continued relevance. This chapter explores Natalie Wood's roles in these two films as well as her faded celebrity during the decade that separates them. These films, in tandem with Wood's public reinvention of herself as someone whose rebel days are far behind her, tell one last chapter of a story about a culture in transition.

Bob & Carol & Ted & Alice is Paul Mazursky's first film as both director and screenwriter. On the heels of his screenwriting debut, *I Love You Alice B. Toklas!* (1968), it cemented his career as a chronicler of, in his terms, the generation 'in between the gap, trying to make certain kinds of transitions and adjustments all the time between the old and the new' (Greenfeld 1970, 55). The idea for the film arose after he and his wife of fifteen years, Betsy (to whom he is still married), attended a weekend at the Esalen Institute, the legendary centre for the Human Potential Movement, and the major therapeutic challenge to Freudian psychoanalysis during the sixties. The Human Potential Movement focused not on mental and emotional sickness but on health and well-being. With such techniques as Gestalt and transactional analysis, it emphasised 'self-help' and introspection in order to reach deeper self-awareness. The Movement's creed focused particularly on sex and the need for guilt-free satisfaction of one's pleasures and desires. Like Bob in the film, Mazursky went there with the intention of developing a documentary on the Movement, but decided to write a screenplay instead. With his partner, Larry Tucker, he improvised a series of set pieces dealing with a 'delicious, pseudo-hip, trendy LA couple' and their decidedly more uptight best friends as they test the waters of group sex and open marriage (Mazursky 1999, 156). The film thus has the rather fluid and even disjunctured feeling of a comedy revue show. Its gently satirical tone and comedic setting create an intimate and low-key atmosphere, far removed from the epic melodramas on forbidden desires that characterised Hollywood's first ventures into the sexual revolution. Still, with its risqué premise and titillating potential, *Bob & Carol & Ted & Alice* became Hollywood's official response to the counterculture, one that appeared on the surface to champion the new open-mindedness but eventually reverted back to a celebration of conventional values around marriage and sexuality.

Wood was the first to be cast in the film. In order to back an untried director, Columbia Pictures insisted on a major star and recommended that Mazursky fly to England to talk with her. Mazursky recalls being quickly enchanted by this beautiful but very nervous woman who not so long ago was the reigning Hollywood box-office queen. Although he was only 'eighty-twenty' sure that she was up to the acting requirements of his new, quirky approach to comedy, he realised that her lack of irony or any sardonic edge to her character created an 'adorable sincerity' that turned into satire despite itself (ibid.). It was precisely because Wood was seen as out of touch, shallow and naive that Mazursky felt that she could carry the deceptively difficult role of Carol Sanders. She is an infuriatingly understanding wife who not only forgives but is actually grateful to her husband for cheating on her. Mazursky chose as her husband the television actor Robert Culp, a slickly handsome leading man who bore an uncanny resemblance to her ex-husband, Robert Wagner. Culp was then starring in the high-style espionage series *I Spy* (1965–8) and was known for his cool, LA attitude. Together, Wood and Culp personified the West Coast wanna-be hipster, 'too old to

With Robert Culp in *Bob & Carol & Ted & Alice*
(1969) (Columbia Pictures/Photofest)

have grown up on marijuana but too young to retire to the golf
course' (Schlesinger, 1969, 118).

With then newcomers Elliott Gould and Dyan Cannon added
as Bob and Carol's neurotic and uptight friends Ted and Alice
Henderson, the film reached a near-perfect balance between Old and
New Hollywood, between the brittle artifice of Hollywood star acting
and the almost achingly casual naturalism of independent cinema.
This is not to suggest that Wood was older than the rest of the cast.
In fact she was, along with Gould, the youngest. Yet, by 1969, Wood
was a twenty-year-plus veteran of Hollywood, while Cannon and
Gould were only just beginning to launch their film careers and were
better known to the New York theatre scene. Given that the film was

in every way about Los Angeles, or what Pauline Kael called 'the middle-class southern California of so much tawdry Americana … a decaying Doris Dayland' (1969, 144) but through a New Yorker's eyes, the film also captures a transitional moment as the film centre of America shifted from the West Coast to the East. With it came a change in sensibilities from the bright-eyed optimism of the Golden State to the gritty realism and highbrow aspirations of an apparently more authentic culture. Thus, the satire of the film comes not only at the expense of Carol Sanders, but also of Natalie Wood, who had embraced all that was under attack by New American Cinema. Her brave performance as a maturing woman who thinks she gets it but who so clearly does not, only works because the actress herself clearly does not get it either. As Mazursky realised, only an actress as naive as the character could pull off the role. Just a hint of neurosis or genuine self-reflection from Carol would quickly derail the plot and remove any trace of believability in the character.

Wood seems to have instinctively realised that the role of Carol was exactly the character expected of her at this juncture in her career. The film arrived at the tail end of six years of half-hearted sexual emancipation, just before she was set to marry a man considerably older than her. After turning down leads in such marquee films as the aforementioned *Bonnie and Clyde*, but also *Barefoot in the Park* (1967) and *Woman Times Seven* (1967), she needed a film that would reintroduce her to the American public as a new-and-improved version of herself, updated for the times but not too drastically. For her return to Hollywood, she decided to abandon what she alternately called The Face, The Badge or The Image: her carefully cultivated, heavily made-up glamour-girl look for which she had often been publicly ridiculed but to which she steadfastly clung (Finstad 2001, 327). In a 1968 article in *Life* magazine entitled 'Glamor Gets the Gate as the "Uglies" Come into Their Own', Wood remained the defender of the old star look. 'Fantasy is dead and it's sad in a way. Just by being pretty all *that* could happen to you

– stardom. Today it still happens – look at Faye Dunaway – but in a real way' (Hallowell 1968, 110). As part of her own updating, Wood adopted a more 'real' version of movie-star beauty, even doing her own make-up on the set and eschewing the usual star trappings of a lavish dressing room dripping with attendants.

Mazursky and the rest of the cast recall with love her lack of 'silly star crap' on the set. Gould proclaims, 'Natalie was not just there as a star, she was there as a fellow human being. Like a sister' (Finstad 2001, 327). The director recalls that she lost control of her new 'real' self only once during filming. Ironically, it was not over her naked exposure on screen but because she felt she was not exposed enough. Toward the end of the film, as Carol and Alice – for very different reasons – try to cajole their husbands into an orgy, Natalie Wood gives a speech to Elliott Gould's character while Robert Culp languorously undresses with Dyan Cannon in the foreground. Wood felt that the audience wouldn't be paying attention to her despite the fact that she was only wearing bra and panties and stormed off the set. When Mazursky spoke to her about how important this film was for everyone, especially since their careers were nowhere near as established as hers, 'the former child star who had been brought up on a diet of conventional movie rights and wrongs showed real class'. She returned and did the scene exactly as planned (Mazursky 1999, 191).

While filming, Wood sat down for an interview with John Hallowell for the *New York Times*, the same journalist who wrote the anti-glamour story for *Life* in which she was called, 'one of the finest examples of the manufactured products'. It was her opportunity to reveal the new honest, authentic version of Natalie Wood – one that would hopefully dispel her reputation as 'Hollywood's favourite Kewpie doll' (Hallowell 1969, D13). She announced the end of her star persona. 'I've done with The Face – you learn you can do it better yourself. There's a time for that, I've had mine.' Speaking about why she chose as her comeback film a quirky comedy with an untried director, she claimed,

It has an underlying sense of what I think is happening in America today with young married people. A kind of searching for deeper honesty underneath the comedy. And the character I play is closer to my own personality than any part I've ever played.

This need to explore her own identity through a new acting challenge was particularly acute for her, as she claimed,

Don't ask me what it's like to be a *star* – because what in God's name does *that* mean? What is it like to be a *person*? I don't have an answer, but I'm working on it. That's what I've been doing, if you want to know.

Wood casually dismissed what she called 'The Star Thing' and the way that Hollywood can turn actors into commodities, yet was careful to not bite the hand that had fed her so long.

But don't think I'm knocking Hollywood, because I'm not. That's a cop-out. If you don't like it, get out. These New Yorkers who come out here and write about terrible, terrible Hollywood. As they're all putting it down, who kills themselves trying to get movie money? (Hallowell 1969, D13)

As if to punctuate her refusal to leave 'The Star Thing' behind completely, Wood carefully constructed her image for this interview, wearing a silver lamé minidress and sable coat and cooing to the crowd that had assembled to watch her play blackjack at a Vegas casino. Even the author notes, 'Natalie has the infuriating morning bloom of a movie star, and the winnings, while the rest of us have the unshaven hangovers, and the losings' (ibid.). The role of Carol fit neatly into Wood's own sense of her significance to Hollywood. Carol, she insisted, was essentially her: they had both enjoyed their sexually rebellious days and were now ready to settle down, but not without a little glamour and daring still in their lives.

This collision of star/actor/person that Wood invokes in this interview is, in many ways, an attempt to reboot her image after spending much of the sixties taunting the press with a deliberately arch façade of Hollywood glamour on speed. Even as early as 1962, the *Saturday Evening Post* called her a 'Hollywood Throwback', and wrote, 'Nothing fazes her in her relentless campaign to be recognized as a movie star in the old flamboyant tradition' (Davidson 1962, 32). More sympathetically, *Good Housekeeping* claimed that Wood wanted three seemingly incompatible life goals: 'to stay at the top in Hollywood, but to become an important actress. At the same time, she has every intention of achieving a satisfying private life as a woman' (Pope 1962, 35). All three eluded her grasp for the rest of the decade. None of her roles after the triumvirate of *Splendor in the Grass*, *West Side Story* and *Gypsy* garnered the same levels of critical or commercial success, while her serial break-ups gobbled up most of the media attention. As a serious actress, she endured the most mockery. Pauline Kael seemed to make it her mission to undermine Wood at every available opportunity, while other journalists would reference her as the ultimate tired Hollywood star cliché (Phelps 1966, 8; Reed 1967, D13).

Perhaps the most scathing critique came from Tom Wolfe, originally written in 1966 and collected in his seminal chronicle of the counterculture, *The Pump House Gang*. In 'The Shockkkkkk of Recognition', Wolfe skewers celebrity culture and the artifice of stardom by recounting an afternoon spent art shopping with Wood. Wolfe puts Wood ahead of Elizabeth Taylor and Marilyn Monroe as the most overwrought and self-constructed star who 'pushed the publicity mill as far as it could go'. Suggesting that her new passion for Impressionism was as shallow as the photograph hounds who wait outside her hotel and that her image was as pretty and empty as the painted sunsets that she proclaims she is 'really hung up on', Wolfe recounts his experience:

those marvellous huge eyes will come out, right here, like a deer's, real, spread open at Clancy, like a surrender, sweet, a child, Natalie here in the dark in Woodhaven, Queens, opening, oh God, come out now, Natalie – *shock* – a celebrity *autograph* … no! a goddess captured … . (1968, 291).

What does not seem apparent to Wolfe or to any of her other critics is that Wood was clearly aware of their smug attitude toward her and toyed with them by vamping the very star characteristics they despised: lavishly out-of-place outfits, ostentatiously long cigarette holders, cooed phrases about 'my darling new Bonnard' (Bart 1966, 45) and an infuriating indifference to their desire to extract a confession of loneliness or self-doubt by appearing almost sickeningly content.

One way to attack Wood's star performance was not simply to critique her admittedly limited acting range, but to hold it up as emblematic of all that was wrong with Hollywood. In her review of *Bob & Carol & Ted & Alice*, Kael remarked,

The whole area of screen acting is probably going to be a big can of worms in the next few years. We are already looking for closer identity between actor and role in many movies; we have become too acute about nuances … to accept the iron-butterfly kind of star acting anymore.

She went on,

The performances that work best force us to a speculative invasion of the privacy of the actors; what would have once seemed gossip is now central not only to the performance but to the conception itself. With the camera coming in closer and closer, the inescapable question is: Can you act it if you're *not* it? (1969, 148).

Kael's answer as far as Wood was concerned was an emphatic 'No.' However, her outmoded acting skills actually help her to bring believability to the role of Carol. The transformations in Hollywood acting that Kael recognises, alongside a major image reconstruction being orchestrated by Wood herself, in a controversial film that received wildly fluctuating reviews, together signal an important juncture in the development of cinematic acting and Hollywood stardom, related to changes in American attitudes around sex and the self. It was a change from a deeply social and edifying imperative to build a cohesive national identity, to a far more individualist concern with happiness under the guise of authenticity and being 'in the now'.

Bob & Carol & Ted & Alice was the Hollywood response to a growing sense that marriage need no longer mean a lifetime of sexual fidelity. However, as Michael DeAngelis argues, it turned a deeply complicated set of social problems related to changes in the economic, medical, social, political and cultural conditions of marriage into a simplistic morality tale to re-assert 'the collective national heterosexual consciousness' (2009, 131). The film tells the story of Bob and Carol, an inexplicably wealthy couple (he's an independent documentary film-maker, she's a stay-at-home mom) who attend a weekend retreat at 'The Institute', a thinly veiled version of Esalen. As Bob and Carol drive their sporty convertible up the canyon to The Institute, the credits roll over shots of nude suntanning, Tai Chi classes and group bathing, with an electric version of Handel's 'Hallelujah Chorus' resounding triumphantly across the landscape. After the weekend, Bob and Carol decide to embark on a journey of 'total honesty' and 'insight' by having sex with anyone they want. They attempt to recruit their best friends, the sexually repressed Alice and the sexually frustrated Ted, to their new lifestyle. During a weekend getaway in Las Vegas to see Tony Bennett perform, Alice discovers that Ted cheated on her. Her response is to dare everyone to prove their openness by having an orgy. After much discussion and a few awkward starts, the two couples realise they can't go through with it. The ending of the film, which caused so many critics to roll their eyes, is an extended Fellini-esque parade set to the tune of Burt Bacharach's 'What the World Needs Now (Is Love, Sweet Love)' as the characters – who now seem to be playing themselves – join forces with the casino crowd to march around a parking lot and stare lovingly into each other's eyes. More than a few critics noted the indebtedness of this ending to Federico Fellini's *8½* (1963), although the intention here isn't distanciation so much as group therapy.

Mazursky directed with a kind of clinical voyeurism. There are almost no full close-ups except those at the beginning and end, which are both tied closely to Encounter sessions, part of the Human Potential Movement's techniques to achieve total openness and honesty. Frequently the camera pans down on the characters, eavesdropping on intimate moments such as when Bob confesses to an affair and Carol is so moved that they have sex in their opulent bathroom, or when Ted, playing in the pool with their kids, admits to Bob that he almost cheated on Alice. The film also makes strategic use of silence, especially in its final ten minutes as the characters fumble toward the failed orgy. There is no doubt that the film is trying to deliver a deeply conventional message about sex, love and marriage at a time when the three were becoming uncoupled. The change from highbrow classical music at the beginning to adult contemporary popular music by the end also signals the absence of high-minded or cerebral pretensions. Sylvia Delgaudio comments on the aural–visual juxtaposition between the opening and closing sequences, suggesting that the film makes a compelling opening statement about 'misplaced faith', but also sets the stage to treat any transformation as ultimately superficial (1992, 186). Critiques that the film is not truly countercultural but is, if anything, a reaction to the counterculture, seem moot since Wood herself offered up the same analysis even before its release. It was, after all, its presentation of conventional marriage as inevitable that appealed to her in the first place.

Vincent Canby of the *New York Times* dismissed it as 'a conventional comedy about the new morality, told in terms of the old, [which] manages to be offensive for the least stimulating of reasons' (1969, 50). Surprisingly, one of the film's biggest supporters was Pauline Kael. To be sure, she spends ample time criticising Wood's acting, suggesting that she 'doesn't seem to have any substance as a human being … she has nothing to draw upon but that same desperate anxiety and forced smile and agitation she's always drawn upon'. However, she has glowing praise for the rest of the cast and especially Mazursky. She notes appreciatively that the director has forged a new, more intimate style of acting derived 'from satiric improvisational revue theatre … and from TV situation comedy, and, with skill and wit, has made this mixture work' (1969, 150). Roger Ebert was similarly sympathetic, recognising that this is a film about

the in-between generation … it understands the peculiar nature of the moral crisis for Americans in this age group, and understands that the way to consider it is in a comedy. What is comedy, after all, but tragedy seen from the outside? (1969)

By casting an actress best known for her over-the-top portrayals of tragic teen heroines nearly undone by their sexual desires, and placing her at the centre of a film that retreads all that fraught territory as farce, *Bob & Carol & Ted & Alice* can be seen as a continuation of Hollywood's forays into changing sexual values without any real intention to be revolutionary.

Although she is clearly struggling in the part, falling back on her star-acting techniques, Wood's failings actually help make her character less ludicrous. She frequently appears scantily but immaturely clad in babydoll pajamas, a bikini, a tennis shirt with no shorts, and bra and panties. She approaches her character as a sexually savvy naïf, offering up sex and Scotch in equal measure to make the men around her feel comfortable. When Bob discovers her in bed with the tennis pro, Carol becomes quintessential Natalie Wood, as she widens her eyes and cocks her head in disbelief at her husband's jealousy. It is difficult not to see at that moment a grown-up Judy or Deanie, or even Susan from *Miracle on 34th Street* as the mannerisms and facial expressions are identical to the ones she's relied on throughout her career. While on the one hand, it exposes her limited acting skills, it also grants a certain kind of pleasure in the comforting predictability and knowability of the actress (Wojcik 2003, 224).

Thus, it is no coincidence that Natalie Wood chose this film to end her self-imposed exile; nor that she justified her choice by freely discussing in the press her own journey of self-discovery and her hopes that it will ultimately lead her to a conventionally domestic happily ever after. Her casting is crucial to offset any potential for sexual excess and signal that this will be a slightly risqué but ultimately safe film about some innocent sexual hi-jinx that will inevitably straighten themselves out. Gould recalls that Wood took on a mentoring role throughout filming so that the less seasoned actors would stay grounded. During the filming of the orgy scene where Mazursky encouraged improvisation, the actors became a bit hysterical. 'There was some degree of manipulation going on for the four of us to physically interact … but the anchor there was Natalie.' In his estimation, 'she was perfect' (Finstad 2001, 327). As Gould claims, Wood took seriously her role as senior actor on set to ensure that nothing went too far that might not only disrupt her image but also lead her into performing something that wasn't true to herself. The important thing is, however, that these are ultimately one and the same thing. The film reveals Wood as a woman who arrived at the sexual revolution and New Hollywood a little too early to really enjoy the party and wants to offer one last defence for the star actor and the not-totally sexually liberated woman.

With a thunderously successful comeback, Wood initially intended to continue acting, even optioning the rights to the book

Bob & Carol & Ted & Alice (1969) (BFI)

I Never Promised You a Rose Garden, and consulting with Kazan to direct her. Once she realised she was pregnant she announced that she was putting acting aside yet again to focus on marriage and motherhood. As she told *Photoplay* about a year after her daughter Natasha was born:

For the first time I feel an inner emotional security. There is reality and dependability. My life revolves around Richard and the baby. I don't have to make endless decisions anymore. Richard is a strong man with integrity and good judgment. He assumes most of the burdens that were once mine. Independence is fine, but not for me (Reynolds 1971, 58).

With that, Wood put aside her reign as Hollywood's most sexually daring ingénue, happily foregoing the sexual independence that her characters had for so long fought a valiant but ultimately losing battle.

Ironically, at the same time as this article hit the newsstands, Wood discovered that Gregson was having an affair with his secretary and she threw him out of the house. By January 1972, her reunion with Robert Wagner had gone public. She spoke candidly to the fan press about her loneliness, her need for someone to love and her optimism for their relationship.

I've been in analysis for a long time and I'm really in touch with my own head now – my feelings. I regret that I didn't seek help when Bob and I still had a chance. Maybe, if we could have grown up a little, we could have stayed married and had our own family (Lawrence 1972, 111).

There is no reference to the contemporary streams of pop psychology in this self-assessment. Rather, it repeats the common motif of 'maturity' demanded by postwar Freudianism, which saw heterosexual domesticity as the pinnacle of psychological health. At a time when divorce rates were skyrocketing and the American family was increasingly being depicted as a besieged, floundering group of disconnected lost souls, cries for more openness, more flexibility and more casual sex seemed a reasonable response for those who had made individualism the cornerstone of domestic harmony (Aldous 1987, 422). But Wood would have none of that. Declaring her total commitment to Wagner months after their second wedding in July 1972, Wood reiterated the same sentiment she had for Gregson just one year prior:

I'll never have to be afraid again! I'll never have that terrible feeling of having to do everything myself, make all my decisions myself, because finally I've found the man who'll protect me from the evil in the world ('Bob & Natalie's Wedding' October 1972, 105).

Until the end of the decade, Wood appeared in only one film, the forgettable *Peeper*, but had a high-profile lead role as Maggie the Cat alongside Wagner's Brick in a televised revival of *Cat on a Hot Tin Roof* for the NBC series, *A Tribute to American Theater* in 1976. Many critics hooted over it as nothing more than a hoary chestnut from an irrelevant era. In the *New York Times* review, the play itself, which had received the Pulitzer Prize in 1955, came under considerable criticism for its weak structure and unconvincing dramatic tension – as if the nation had moved on from its themes of repressed sexuality and unravelling family bonds (O'Connor 1976, 133). Even before the teleplay was released, Wood was deemed a relic of that era of sexual hysteria and an icon of outmoded Hollywood histrionics. In a 1974 article on film acting in the *New York Times*, Urjo Kareda argued that the intensely naturalist performance style currently favoured required a measured, delicate approach in order to create a bond between actor and audience, in contrast to the bombastic, bigger-than-life approach required by classical star-acting. While he had some appreciation for 'good' star-actors like Bette Davis, he singled out Natalie Wood as a quintessentially 'bad' star-actor – despite the fact that she hadn't appeared in a movie in over five years. He wrote:

A bad film actress like Natalie Wood is also likely to send out signals, but something will be amiss. Either she will beep out promises of more drama than she can deliver, or more acting than we want. She can also signal a staggering into the borderlands where self-awareness becomes self-consciousness. Miss Wood's signaling – and hers was always a busy signal – tended to be a frown, an intense knitting of the forehead which always anticipated but never quite delivered some unburdening of psychic truths (Kareda 1974, 11).

Reviews of both *Cat on a Hot Tin Roof* and *Peeper* made reference to her heavy make-up as evidence of her out-of-fashion acting and reliance on physical beauty over psychological complexity in her performance style (Cuskelly 1975; O'Connor 1976, 133). Yet,

With Robert Wagner in *Cat on a Hot Tin Roof*
(1976) (NBC/Photofest)

for all the scathing derision heaped upon her, there was still at least a nostalgic appreciation for the kind of acting and the sorts of roles that Wood personified in less elitist circles. *TV Guide* called her Maggie the Cat 'the performance of her career' and she was nominated for an Emmy (Finstad 2001, 347). The San Francisco Film Festival paid tribute to their hometown girl two months before the broadcast of *Cat on a Hot Tin Roof* with a retrospective of her films and a Q&A session that led to two standing ovations. With such forms of validation, it was possible for her and Wagner to establish themselves as the keepers of the Hollywood flame, acting as Marshalls for the Hollywood Santa Claus parade, hosting parties where the old guard could mingle with new arrivals or dining regularly at the most popular restaurant in town, La Scala. Wagner himself always insisted on a degree of formality in their entertaining to hark back to the 'old days of the balls and parties of the Hollywood I'd known as a young man' (Wagner 2008, 341). Karl Malden remembers them as 'a wonderful Hollywood couple ... they performed properly for the profession, at all sorts of affairs' (Finstad 2001, 347). George Segal concurs, 'Nobody else had Natalie's pizzazz, and the Wagner parties were really an extension of the George Cukor times, with the same mix of younger and older people, the same intelligence and glitter' (Lambert 2004, 267). Wood and Wagner radiated a down-to-earth simplicity as a couple of 'middle-aged squares' who had left the outrageousness of stardom behind but retained its sense of gracious privilege and love of glamour (Berges 1979, 45). Central to that image was the foregrounding of a devoted marriage, unspoiled children and a welcoming home.

In place of film stardom, Wood became a celebrity icon of bourgeois serenity by re-introducing herself as an interior designer. In the seventies, Wood became a familiar face in family and home magazines. In 1976, *House Beautiful* showcased Wood's decorating skills with a six-page spread of her Hollywood Hills home. The house had a deliberately warm, lived-in feeling with a particular emphasis on giving children 'the run of it'. A cacophony of floral and plaid prints, country classic furniture, with throw pillows and accent rugs everywhere would make this home look like any other suburban family dwelling of the seventies, except for the original French Impressionist paintings and American West sculptures, not to mention the dazzling Hollywood memorabilia scattered throughout (Dektar 1976, 51–7). In a similar feature, *Good Housekeeping* claimed 'This comfortable, spacious home is helping the Wagners create the kind of life they've always wanted for themselves and their children' ('At Home with Natalie Wood and Robert Wagner' 1976, 134). Putting her private life on display through features in family and home magazines was part of the work of maintaining Natalie Wood while she was not on screen. Thus that private life, however real to her, was part of a complex performance of identity construction at both conscious and subconscious levels. In these strategic representations of herself as 'happy, comfortable and well-adjusted' (Berges 1979, 42), Wood was not merely commenting on her own happiness. She was also paying tribute to the Hollywood system and the postwar culture that had served her so well but was now under heavy attack from both right and left political sides. This is especially acute in her response to the feminist movement, siding with second-wave early liberal politics rather than the radical-cultural strains that were reverberating by the mid-seventies. In a 1974 article, and again in 1979, she spoke favourably about a movement that allowed women to choose between a career and family. However, she did not want to do away with old-fashioned chivalry like having a man light your cigarette. More importantly, she did not believe that it was possible to have both a career and family, disparaging day-care centres and stating that 'I don't think [having a child and a job] is being responsible and it isn't necessarily being liberated either' (Loewell 1974, 25; Korba 1979, 15).

As if trying to prove herself right, Wood made frequent public claims that acting was no longer important to her and that she would only act if it in no way interfered with her responsibilities to her family. The *Los Angeles Herald Examiner* wrote, 'For the first time since her fourth birthday being an actress is not the primary goal of her life. She'd rather be Mrs. Wagner, wife, mother and homebody, than Ms Wood, glamorous, globe-trotting, headline-grabbing movie star' (Cuskelly 1974, E1). Others took a rather less generous approach to her placid contentment, speculating 'And then there are [celebrities] like Natalie Wood whose public lives appear so banal that the question is not what the "real" Natalie Wood is like but whether there is one' (Loewell 1974, 22). Her refusal of an enigmatic, elusive identity; her willingness to openly discuss her psychoanalysis; her unconditional love for her children; her devotion and subservience to her husband; her contented memories of Old Hollywood and her child-star days all felt somehow 'unreal' in an era of neurotic individualism. Yet Wood stuck doggedly to the poised professionalism trained into her by the studios since her childhood and rebuffed any criticisms of being out of step with the times. She never hesitated to display her overwhelming happiness and her indebtedness to those apparently repressive and inauthentic systems – Hollywood, strict parents, traditional psychoanalysis – that had brought her to this point in her life. As her friend Tommy Thompson wrote in a 1975 profile for *Cosmopolitan*, 'Hers was the familiar Hollywood story: stardom, marriage, divorce, then downhill on Seconals, sycophants, and depression. But Natalie finally said to hell with that script, I like beautiful endings …' (1975, 124).

However, beautiful endings were increasingly less a part of the American prestige cinema experience. In an era of Scorsese, Coppola, Cimino, Friedkin and Bogdanovich, Hollywood in particular and Los Angeles in general appeared as an artificial, artistically vapid space that offered little in the way of authentic insight (Biskind 1998). The travails of a happily married, financially well-off stay-at-home mom enjoying a secluded life in the expensive suburbs of that once-golden city, now beleaguered by corruption, crime and environmental crises were decidedly out of touch. More insightful portraits of women at middle age were available in films like *Alice Doesn't Live Here Anymore* (1974), about a young working-class widow trying to launch a singing career; *Looking for Mr. Goodbar* (1978), about a New York schoolteacher seeking violent, anonymous sex; or even Paul Mazursky's new take on middle-class life, *An Unmarried Woman* (1978), featuring Jill Clayburgh as a forty-something Manhattan matron forced to remake herself after her husband leaves her.

The place to tell stories that resonated with Wood's life was on television and, if on film, through a lighthearted televisual aesthetic. Molly Haskell argues that the difference between film and television is 'between distance and familiarity, between the white heat of the affair and the enduring virtues (or nagging tedium, as the case may be) of marriage'. She continued in a somewhat sympathetic bent, '[television] actors give new life to old forms, and bring an old-fashioned sense of character to modern life' (1979, D32). Certainly, Robert Wagner found his greatest successes on television, first with *It Takes a Thief* (1968–70), later with *Colditz* (1972–4), *Switch* (1975–8) and then *Hart to Hart* (1979–84). He sensed earlier than many that the cool complacency of a man fully satisfied with a life of grace and glamour resonated far better in the living room than in the theatre, and he encouraged his wife to do the same. She turned down the role of Daisy in *The Great Gatsby* (1974) to appear alongside Wagner in the 1973 made-for-television movie *The Affair*, co-produced by Aaron Spelling (Finstad 2001, 341). She even parodied herself as a movie star in a special episode of *Hart to Hart*, playing a spoiled has-been star named Natasha Gurdin. The Wagners used their Hollywood appeal to negotiate a business arrangement with Spelling that gave them a stake in his next series. That series was *Charlie's Angels*, which secured for them the lavish lifestyle befitting two ageing stars.

When, by the end of the seventies, Wood began to seek out acting opportunities again, her first efforts were prestige television events. The miniseries *From Here to Eternity* (1979) reiterates Wood's value to projects in a similar vein to *Cat on a Hot Tin Roof*. Both were remakes of fifties Hollywood films chronicling the sexual angst of the age in largely covert and glossified terms. Both remakes were touted for taking these well-worn stories and removing the veil of coyness in which Hollywood had previously shrouded them. Indeed, to the delight of the media, Wood appeared in a nude scene for *From Here to Eternity* (later excised by NBC). The roles which she reprises were made iconic by Elizabeth Taylor (Maggie the Cat) and Deborah Kerr (Karen Holmes), but also reference a generic character for which she was best known: the sexually frustrated ingénue. In that sense, then, Natalie Wood's casting enhances their nostalgic appeal and the era that they evoke, as well as the forgotten modes of feminine star appeal which she represents. The nostalgic medium of television was a much more welcoming place for this ageing Hollywood beauty.

Despite these successes, Wood was not interested in becoming a television curiosity but sought to regain the stature that came with movie stardom. However, the best roles eluded her so she settled on the romantic comedy *The Last Married Couple in America*, co-starring a family friend, George Segal, and with a roster of television actors rounding out the supporting roles: Valerie Harper (*Mary Tyler Moore* [1970–7] and *Rhoda* [1974–8]), Alan Arbus *(M*A*S*H* [1972–83], Richard Benjamin (*Quark* [1977]) and perennial sitcom guest actor Bob Dishy. The film was directed by Gil Cates, best known for his work on television movies and later as the producer of that greatest of television spectacles, the Academy Award broadcasts. It is therefore not surprising that the film adopts a televisual aesthetic with well-worn but not particularly well-known faces. The film arrived during a downturn in Hollywood's love affair with the special-effects blockbuster and an interest in 'moviegoers in the over-21 bracket who never go disco-roller skating … let's call them "grown ups"' (Maslin 1979, 59). It also marks a growing public dissatisfaction with the purported success of the sexual revolution

The Last Married Couple in America (1980)
(Columbia/Photofest)

and a revived call for a return to the traditional family. This film
about a happily married couple who are reluctantly pushed out of
their complacent life only to rush back in and barricade the doors
of their modern-yet-comfortable home high up in the Los Angeles
canyons, can be seen as the ultimate backlash against the excesses
of the Me Decade (Wolfe 1976).

The film chronicles a brief marital crisis between Jeff and Mari
Thompson. He is a successful architect in the vein of Mike Brady
while she is a stay-at-home mom and sculptor. After realising that
all their close friends have divorced, and under pressure from a
sexually voracious divorcée (Harper) and a Ron Jeremy-like porn
star (Dom DeLuise), they separate and embark on a series of
sexual misadventures intended to make the other person jealous.
A particularly debauched house party and a creepy attempt at

seduction by a swinger couple send the Thompsons rushing back into each other's arms. Mari and Jeff reunite as she asks plaintively, 'How did we ever let those other people get into our lives?' Jeff responds with an ongoing theme of the film, 'Ohhh, police strikes, women's lib, gay lib, condominiums.' The tone is gentle and half-mocking, but the message nonetheless remains the same: the family unit, unperturbed by social restlessness and sexual ferment, is the only 'haven in a heartless world' (Lasch 1977). The point is driven home by the finale, as the Thompsons kick everyone out of their house, wake up their kids and head to a drive-in burger joint for some honest family fun. The closing credits roll to a theme song about how 'we could have it all' that is as saccharine and literal-minded as the one for *Bob & Carol & Ted & Alice*.

The straightforwardness of the conclusion, in which the family is left unscathed and hermetically sealed off from the outside forces who desire its destruction, replicates the routinised structure of the television sitcom: a cohesive, domesticated unit is temporarily destabilised from without in humorous and therefore not really threatening ways before harmony is inevitably restored. Despite its standard widescreen ratio, the film feels like a television episode, shot for the most part in middle view with few close-ups, and none particularly tight. When the camera cranes up to take in the vista, it remains doggedly focused on the married couple on the ground, an island in a sea of nothingness. The comedic action emphasises slapstick bodies more than interior psyches resulting in a dearth of deep dramatic tension and little emotional identification with the characters. Indeed, with the far-fetched premise that drives this otherwise normal, everyday couple apart and then catapult them back together again, the film enacts the same tension between realist settings, naturalist acting and broad comedic performance that characterises the television sitcom (Mills 2005, 68). Thus, in perhaps her final gesture of art imitating life, the presence of Natalie Wood as the decidedly not-with-it matron who realises before it's too late that marriage is an institution worth preserving in its traditional mode makes the unbelievability of the film all too believable. It was a role she had been preparing for all her life.

In an interview with the *New York Times* to promote *The Last Married Couple in America*, Wood once again laid bare the similarities between her character and her real life. 'When you're married these days, you sometimes feel like you're in the wilderness. ... You know, you feel you're the pioneers and the Indians are all around, shooting you down one by one' (Klemesrud 1980, 58). Throughout 1979, as Wood sought to raise her profile by giving as many interviews in that one year as she had since her daughter Courtney was born, the theme was consistent: 'mother and housewife first, and then an actress' (Lardine 1979, 22). However, that rally cry was more muted than it had been in the years when her career lay dormant. Now, she was struggling to perform a delicate balancing act between loving wife, devoted mother and ambitious career woman. Having treated her marriage and children as the latest in a series of roles which required total dedication, the strain of juggling competing roles and proving to herself, as well as to her audiences, that it could be done, sometimes showed through the bravado. In an article in *McCall's*, she hesitantly conceded, 'Work without a family and children isn't very satisfying. But having one shouldn't mean you can't have the other. I finally faced up to the fact that I wanted all of it' (See 1979, 24). In another interview that year she reflected,

My life has been sort of reversed. I was working when other girls were going to school – and when other women were reaching the age where they wanted careers I was most interested in staying at home. Now I want to do a little of both (Thompson 1979, 21).

It would, however, be going too far to suggest that Wood's very public embrace of marriage and motherhood, both off and on screen, was a reactionary throwback to traditionalism. Rather, Wood sought to position herself as an exemplar of that liberal ideal of 'having it all'. Her star turn in *The Last Married Couple in America* was in many ways the companion piece to *Bob & Carol & Ted & Alice*. It incorporated many trademark Wood-isms – especially the wide-eyed, cocked-head look when sexually challenged. However, within the televisual frame of the later film, where close emotional intensity is replaced by a comfortable middleness, Wood's subdued form of star-acting once again delivers the necessary naivety and charming innocence required. As Canby notes, 'She not only looks terrific, she's extremely funny when she's not required to supply emotional bridges left out of the screenplay' (1980, C12). In other words, Wood never lets the audience forget that it is Natalie Wood, lifelong ambassador of American sexual liberalism and chatelaine of Hollywood's most golden family, defending marriage. Indeed, *L'Officiel* argued that, with Natalie Wood in the lead, it was almost certain that *The Last Married Couple in America* would 'set the trend for the return of marriage and family to the American scene' ('Natalie Wood' 1980, 119). As if on cue, the film's release in 1980 coincided with a levelling out of divorce rates along with bitter denunciations of the sexual revolution and laments that the nation had been led into a 'sexual wilderness' (Packard 1970). The message was repeated over and over: women could potentially 'have it all' if they put it all in the correct order, with the family coming first and themselves coming last. To do otherwise would risk their own self-destruction. It was a lesson that Wood taught film audiences for over three decades. Tragically, it was also the final narrative of her life.

After *The Last Married Couple in America*, Wood did something which she publicly vowed she would never do. She accepted a role that would take her away from her family for an extended period of time. That decision reflects the fact that, as her biographers claim, this was a period of frustration when Wood doubted her relevance as either star, actor or person. The film was *Brainstorm* (1983), co-starring Christopher Walken. It would turn out to be her last film, and a far from fitting tribute to her legendary status. Her role in the film is largely secondary to Walken and the special effects, but nonetheless shares a connection to her previous work of this era, in its allegorical commitment to marital fidelity and romantic love. Wood plays Karen Brace, the estranged wife of Michael Brace (Walken), and together they invent a neuro-interface that allows a person's emotional and sensorial experiences to be recorded and re-experienced by another. Through such an exchange, Michael is able to express his true feelings toward her and they reconcile. However, their colleagues use the device for less ennobling purposes, such as intense orgasms and military intelligence (sexual pleasure and state torture metaphorically linked as detrimental to the national good). Eventually, they manage to shut the system down but not before Michael experiences death through the memories of another colleague, replete with interstellar angels irresistibly drawn to a tunnel of bright light. Karen's hysterical grief over Michael's lifeless body is reminiscent of her similar performance in *West Side Story*, and indicative of her limitations. Shot mostly in the dark, and relying heavily on her voice while the cosmic dreamscape floats on, Wood sounds more like a wife impatiently waiting for her husband to start the car, intoning unconvincingly over and over, 'We had a deal!' Without close-ups, Wood struggles to convey emotion. Instead, her thin, strained voice is left alone to carry the final emotional weight of an already weighed-down film.

By the time shooting started, the director, Douglas Trumbull, had lost control over his two stars, who egged each other on to take their roles into their own hands. For Walken, this led to all kinds of indulgences and hamming. For Wood, who depended heavily on strong-willed, intellectual directors to elicit her best, the result is a flat, insecure performance disconnected from the other actors. Yet, by all accounts, Walken was enchanted with Wood and encouraged her to push back against the star façade and focus on her acting. As the tragic events of her death reveal, in the end Wood could not

With Christopher Walken and Douglas Trumbull
on the set of *Brainstorm* (1983) (MGM/UA
Entertainment Company/Photofest)

reconcile her professional commitments as an actor as well as she did
her commitments as a star and still maintain the fairytale family life
that had become her last great performance. Over Thanksgiving,
with production on the troubled set shut down, Walken accompanied
Wood and Wagner on a cruise through the Catalina Islands aboard
their yacht, *Splendour*. The tense relationships on board triggered a
nightmarish argument between the two men over whether Wood
should put her family first or her career. Embarrassed and angry,
Wood stormed out. The next morning, her lifeless body was found
floating in a cove. A lifeguard who assisted in lifting her out of the
water recalled, 'All I remember is her eyes' (ibid., 420).

CONCLUSION: THE ETERNAL INGÉNUE

Some years after her death, Henry Jaglom, the last of Wood's New York Bad Boyfriends from the sixties, commented wistfully, 'What the world missed was one more portrait in this very very empty gallery of portraits of what women are really like at different stages in their lives' ('The Last Studio Star' 1997). While events leading up to Natalie Wood's death remain as murky as the waters in which she drowned, over the years the legend that has grown up around them has only helped to cement her legacy as the tragic heroine caught in a maelstrom of competing sexual values. In a eulogy of sorts, John Tibbetts summed up her career as 'a gradual "coming of age" for both her and for Hollywood cinema in general' (Tibbetts 1982, 30). Perhaps that is why Wood is not remembered as central to her best-known films nor spoken of with the same reverence as Monroe or Taylor. She could never fill up the screen as fully as they did, nor invoke the same unattainable desirability required of a screen goddess. While Monroe and Taylor seem to encapsulate a distinct moment in Hollywood history, Wood appears in the gaps, margins and fissures of that same history. Her career exemplifies the tensions of America cinema in transition: the demise of the studio system and the rise of the independent actor; challenges to Hollywood star-acting from intense psychoanalytical models such as Method acting; and the loosening of censorship regulations coupled with audience demands for more explicit depictions of the socio-sexual crises affecting the nation. Yet it also speaks to the ambivalence that continues to affect women's roles today, as Hollywood still uneasily tests the boundaries of women's sexual independence and wilfully omits depictions of sexually mature women (Ogilvie 2015; Smith and Cook 2008).

Wood benefited in many ways as a member of the 'in-between generation'. She underscored the moments just before or just after a major cultural revolution rather than a culture at its height. It is little surprise, then, how much she frustrated critics who could never decide what to say about her:

'The girl is a superb actress.'
'She couldn't act her way out of a wet paper bag.'
'She's gorgeous.'
'She's a plain, bony little broad, with too much makeup and no bust.'
'She's bright as hell – takes courses at UCLA, collects art, and speaks Russian like Brezhnev.'
'I've talked to smarter fence posts.'
'She's easy to work with.'
'She's impossible, always throwing her weight around' (Whitman 1967, 31).

In many ways, all these statements are true as Wood's only real consistency was her unevenness and indecisiveness. Wood was not a great actress on her own, but was capable of great performances when given the necessary tools of script, direction and co-star. That is not to belittle her accomplishments or detract from her importance. Rather, it is to reflect upon the ways that acting is not a natural gift but demands intensive commitment and hard work, with success never guaranteed. No one ever faulted Wood for her determination and tenacity, even if they mocked her for the imperfect results.

In reviewing her long and tumultuous career, one final aspect becomes clear: Wood's star status is cemented not so much by her but by the importance of her films and, more crucially, her male directors and co-stars. Three of Wood's star-billing films also mark the debut of men who ultimately outstripped her iconicity: *Rebel Without a Cause* (James Dean), *Splendor in the Grass* (Warren Beatty) and *Inside Daisy Clover* (Robert Redford). While her secondary status could be explained away as the simple fact that her co-stars were ultimately more talented and charismatic than her, there is nonetheless a nagging sense that Hollywood never really gave her the chance to be at the centre of her own narrative. No film demonstrates such a lack of commitment to its star as *Inside Daisy Clover*. It should have proven that Wood was capable of making the transition to New Hollywood. Instead, due to directorial choices not communicated to Wood, it left her in the lurch while her co-star went on to become one of the biggest stars of the next generation (Mordden 1990, 79). This book concludes with an examination of the film that silenced Wood so much that her career never quite recovered.

Written by Gavin Lambert (her later biographer) and produced-directed by Alan Pakula and Richard Mulligan (*To Kill a Mockingbird* [1962], and *Love with the Proper Stranger*), *Inside Daisy Clover* mocks Hollywood and sexual convention in equally insufficient doses. Wood plays the titular lead, 'a primitive child, adult beyond her years, a rebel with a cause' (*Inside Daisy Clover*, PCA Analysis of Film Content 9 November 1965). Although she was twenty-seven, her character is only fifteen when the film begins and seventeen when it ends. Daisy is a combination street urchin/ flower child, roaming the boardwalks of Angel Beach at the height of the Depression. After recording a song for a talent contest, Daisy is whisked to Hollywood by a mercurial studio boss, Raymond Swan (Christopher Plummer). As he molds her into a vulgar caricature of the spectacular orphan, his other hot property, matinee idol Wade Lewis (Robert Redford) goads her into a rebellion that culminates in their elopement and his immediate desertion. She discovers from Swan's wife, who was also

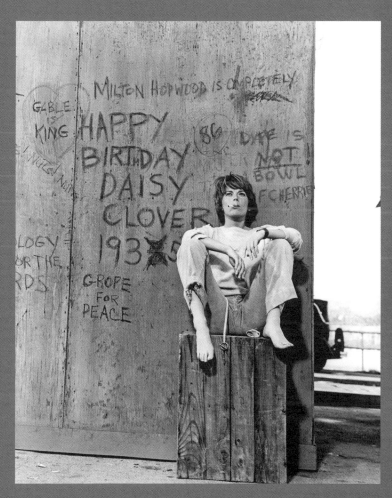

Inside Daisy Clover (1965) (BFI)

having an affair with Wade, that he is a homosexual. Daisy rebounds into an affair with Swan, who rewards her by reuniting her with her mother and giving them an isolated seaside cottage in which to live. After her mother dies, Daisy suffers a nervous breakdown in the recording booth of a sound stage. Back in the cottage, as she lies in bed, stubbornly silent, all her handlers visit her to cajole her back to work. The only line she speaks out loud is to Swan: 'My hair is going grey.' To which he chuckles, 'My grey-haired teenager.' The film ends when Daisy sets fire to the house and storms off merrily down the beach. When a passerby asks what happened she replies, 'Somebody declared war.' As she flits along, skirting the edges of the screen, she suddenly shifts into the centre and the film freezes. Rather than showing that she has escaped her Hollywood captors, this final image has her imprisoned by the film; going neither forward nor backward but merely stuck in between, much like Wood was herself throughout her career.

The sixties were not kind to its actresses, argues Ethan Mordden. Angst-fuelled introspection was for hustlers and loners. Women, apparently, could be neither and so were accessories to the male protagonists and easily abandoned by the plot (ibid., 77). Wexman calls this the 'companionate model' of Hollywood romance in which women were to be independent but not competitive. That characterisation extended to the actual actresses who were expected to hold their own on screen but only to the point that they initiated their co-stars' emotional journey and did not try to hog the picture for themselves (1993, 145). Mordden points out that, rather than proof of her limitations, it was a unique talent of Wood's to bring star power to a film while generously sharing the screen with her unknown co-star. She projected a

go-everywhere freshness amazing in someone who had been in movies without a break since 1943. ... The point is made: she is vulnerable because every man wants her. This is about as strong a position as a woman star could hold in the 1960s (1990, 78).

The final freeze frame of *Inside Daisy Clover* (1965)

In *Inside Daisy Clover*, Wood is desired by her two male leads, but is valued more for her commercial appeal. After her nervous breakdown, her lover-employer viciously demands she get out of bed and 'make me money!' Even Wade beseeches her at the end 'won't you join me back in the limelight, little lady of pain?' In that sense, the film traverses the two major journeys of Wood's life: child into star and child into woman (Lawrence 2001, 225). Perhaps that is why Wood so desired this role, and why the producers could think of no one else to play it. Lambert recalls that Wood told him, 'I'd kill for this part.' He responded, 'Don't bother, you're the first choice of everyone concerned' (2004, 219).

If *Rebel Without a Cause* was about her own confused teenage rebellion, and *The Last Married Couple in America* was about her midlife crisis, then *Inside Daisy Clover*, coming at the middle of her career, is about her ambivalent relationship to her stardom. Curiously, Wood is once again expected to sing and dance for this role, despite the fact that she had already demonstrated minimal talent there in both *West Side Story* and *Gypsy*. The studios didn't even try to hide the fact that Wood's singing was dubbed by Marni Noxon in the former, and overdubbed in the latter, while her dance sequences were as limited as possible for the star of a musical. Wexman points out that it was not unusual to expect leading actresses to sing and dance, allowing the viewers to revel in their beauty while underscoring the hard work of stardom (1993, 145). Pullen suggests that this kind of spectacular performance demanded of women was in fact deeply invested in naturalist acting traditions to showcase both their inherent dazzlingness as well as their intense desire to please (2014, 15). Amy Lawrence suggests that by giving Daisy a natural ability to sing – 'I just open my mouth and a song comes out' – sidesteps the character's right to any narrative voice and grants her only an 'emotionally expressive voice' (2001, 223). I take that argument one step further and insist that by cleverly masking Wood's voice during the scenes when she is supposed to be singing, *Inside Daisy Clover* denies Wood both voices.

Many have commented that the Daisy Clover in the novel is reminiscent of Judy Garland, especially since it concludes with her leaving Hollywood to become a concert singer in New York (Feuer 1992, 120; Levy 2009). There are comparisons with Garland's own comeback film *A Star Is Born* (1954), in which she is discovered by Hollywood after she belts out 'The Man Who Got Away' during an after-hours jam session with her band. In contrast, Wood's Daisy is never shown as a natural singer but is only heard singing in a film studio. The fact that the film cannot convincingly show Wood breaking out into song except when she is being filmed layers on the artifice as Wood the actor-who-can't-sing plays an actor-who-can-sing-but-doesn't. Her singing isn't heard when she is being recorded, only when she is being filmed and the dubbing in those scenes is intentionally obvious. In the opening montage, Wood enters a penny-arcade recording booth and presumably sings the song which launches her to stardom. Even this isn't certain because the scene is shot in silhouette from outside the booth and she is only seen snapping her fingers and mouthing words that are presumed to be song. In the climactic scene, Daisy is again locked in a recording booth to overdub her singing but she is unable to synchronise with her on-screen self. The camera closes in on her frantically trying to sing but no sound is heard until she becomes hysterical. As Swan throws open the door and forcibly controls her, she roars frantically but to no end other than her complete collapse. Thus Wood's 'emotionally expressive voice' isn't even one of natural talent, but of total loss of control and capitulation to men stronger than her.

Inside Daisy Clover was supposed to include at least thirty different voiceovers, divulging the character's inner thoughts as she is used and manipulated by almost everyone in the film except, perhaps, her half-senile mother (Ruth Gordon). Wood recorded them all, and thus played all her scenes as if a narration was going on behind her silent gestures. On the set, Mulligan treated her much like Kazan and Ray had, with many private sessions and intense consultations about how she viewed the character. She also clicked personally and professionally with Redford, making the love story between them charming and poignant instead of creepy and abusive (Swan even remarks when they announce their affair that he could have him arrested since Daisy is under age). Indeed, Wood felt that the film 'seemed to be going dangerously well' and would propel her back into serious-actor territory (Lambert 2004, 224). Then she secretly attended a rough-cut premiere of the film and realised that she had been betrayed. Without telling her, Pakula and Mulligan removed all the voiceovers except for those at the beginning and the end. The result is that Wood seems to be over-acting with her eyes and tilting head while she remains perversely, frustratingly silent. The voiceovers were never reinstated, causing Wood to utter defeatedly, 'It was like cutting out half my performance' (ibid.). Between that and the freeze-frame ending, the film doesn't critique what Hollywood does to its women but seems to settle in for a long ride of silencing and immobilising. Somewhat prophetically, in 1962, a fan magazine wrote:

What it boils down to is that Hollywood almost destroyed Natalie Wood during her childhood. And, although she's riding high at the moment, it might well destroy her in the future. The star system does brutal things to women (Pope 1962, 35).

Did the star system kill Natalie Wood? Did it even brutalise her? Or did it save her when the demands of New Hollywood acting proved beyond her emotional and intellectual reach? As one interviewer wrote, '"Daisy is basically a survivor," Natalie says. And so is she, Natalie!' (Clein 1970, 9). It wasn't until the end of her life that she could be appreciated for all that she had done for American cinema, filling in the spaces between a transitioning Hollywood and a society in uproar. That she played this role for almost her entire life and ended up 'sensible, functioning, productive, one of the more responsible members of her industry, an able worker in the vineyards of civic endeavor, and a contender for the most beautiful woman in town' brought renewed faith that maybe women could have it all (Thompson 1979, 10). Wood herself seemed to believe it was finally possible, saying:

For women a career and a family have often been an either/or proposition. Either you had a career or you got married and had kids. And it was always very difficult to blend the two. Whether it was true or not, that's the way it was always presented. But now, with the changing role of women, I think people are beginning to realize you can have both, that you can be a good wife and mother and pursue a career at the same time. I'm glad the rigidity of that kind of old-fashioned thinking is changing (Land 1979, 84).

Instead, Wood became the tragedy she had worked so hard to avoid. In an effort to create some narrative sense of her death, a journalist surmised, 'However, something was missing. She drank more, took more pills, and longed for a film comeback. Her remarks: "I need more than this. I need a good film role," and "You know what I want?

I want yesterday"' (Sheppard 1988, 11). This tossing between past and future, contentment and restlessness speaks to how she more than anyone else expressed women's ongoing conflicts to find their rightful place in post-studio American cinema, often confounding those who wanted to write the script for her. Wood, therefore, deserves to be remembered by some of her own last words, 'I am a woman, a wife, a mother, and a working actress' (Thompson 1979, 13).

Natalie Wood (1969) (Photofest)

BIBLIOGRAPHY

Aldous, Joan, 'American Families in the 1980s: Individualism Run Amok?', *Journal of Family Issues* vol. 8 no. 4 (December 1987), pp. 422–5.

Anderson, Lisa M., *Mammies No More: The Changing Image of Black Women on Stage and Screen* (Lanham, MD: Rowman & Littlefield Publishers, Inc., 1997).

Arbiser, Samuel, *On Freud's 'Inhibitions, Symptoms and Anxiety'* (London: Karnac Books, 2013).

Baer, William, 'On Rebel Without a Cause: A Conversation with Stewart Stern', *Michigan Quarterly Review* vol. 38 no. 4 (Fall 1999), pp. 580–604. HTML version, n.p. Accessed 22 August 2011.

Bailey, Beth L., *From Front Porch to Back Seat: Courtship in Twentieth-century America* (Baltimore, MD: Johns Hopkins University Press, 1988).

Bailey, Beth L., *Sex in the Heartland* (Cambridge, MA: Harvard University Press, 1999).

Baker, Carroll, *Baby Doll: An Autobiography* (Westminster, MD: Arbor House, 1983).

Balcerzak, Scott, 'Dickensian Orphan as Child Star: Freddie Bartholomew and the Commodity of Cute in MGM's David Copperfield (1935)', *Film Literature Quarterly* vol. 33 no. 1 (2005), pp. 51–61.

Baron, Cynthia and Sharon Marie Carnicke, *Reframing Screen Performance* (Ann Arbor: University of Michigan Press, 2008).

Biskind, Peter, *Easy Riders, Raging Bulls: How the Sex, Drugs, and Rock'N'Roll Generation Saved Hollywood* (New York: Simon & Schuster, 1998).

Breines, Wini, *Young, White and Miserable: Growing Up Female in the Fifties* (Chicago, IL: University of Chicago Press, 2001).

Buscombe, Edward, *The Searchers* (London: BFI, 2000).

Butler, Jeremy, *Star Texts: Image and Performance in Film and Television* (Detroit, MI: Wayne State University Press, 1991).

Courtney, Susan, *Hollywood Fantasies of Miscegenation: Spectacular Narratives of Gender and Race, 1903–1967* (Princeton, NJ: Princeton University Press, 2004).

Dean, Virgil W., *An Opportunity Lost: The Truman Administration and the Farm Policy Debate* (Kansas City: University of Missouri Press, 2006).

DeAngelis, Michael, 'Mispronouncing "Man and Wife": The Fate of Marriage in Hollywood's Sexual Revolution', in Sean Griffin (ed.), *Hetero: Queering Representations of Straightness* (Albany: SUNY Press, 2009), pp. 129–49.

Delgaudio, Sylvia, 'Columbia and the Counterculture: Trilogy of Defeat', in Bernard F. Dick (ed.), *Columbia Pictures: Portrait of a Studio* (Lexington: University Press of Kentucky, 1992), pp. 182–90.

Deutsch, Helene, *The Psychology of Women: A Psychoanalytic Interpretation* (New York: Grune & Stratton, 1944).

Doane, Mary Ann, *Femmes Fatales: Feminism, Film Theory and Psychoanalysis* (New York: Routledge, 1991).

Doherty, Thomas, *Teenagers & Teenpics: The Juvenilization of American Movies in the 1950s* (Boston, MA: Unwin Hyman, 1988).

Douglas, Susan J., *Where the Girls Are: Growing Up Female with the Mass Media* (New York: Times Books, 1994).

Douvan, Elizabeth and Joseph Adelson, *The Adolescent Experience* (New York: John Wiley & Sons, Inc., 1966).

Dyer, Richard, *White* (New York: Routledge, 1997).

Dyer, Richard, *The Matter of Images: Essays on Representation*, 2nd edn (New York: Routledge, 2002).

Dyer, Richard, *Heavenly Bodies: Film Stars and Society* (New York: Routledge, 2003).

Eisenschitz, Bernard, *Nicholas Ray: An American Journey*, trans. Tom Milne (London: Faber and Faber, 1993).

Feuer, Jane, *The Hollywood Musical*, 2nd edn (Bloomington: Indiana University Press, 1992).

Foster, Gwendolyn Audrey, *Performing Whiteness: Modern Re/constructions in the Cinema* (Albany: SUNY Press, 2003).

Frascella, Lawrence and Al Weisel, *Live Fast, Die Young: The Wild Ride of Making Rebel Without a Cause* (New York: Simon & Schuster, 2005).

Gabbard, Krin, *Jammin' at the Margins: Jazz and the American Cinema* (Chicago, IL: University of Chicago Press, 1996).

Gans, Herbert J., 'The Rise of the Problem-Film: An Analysis of Changes in Hollywood Films and the American Audience', *Social Problems* vol. 11 no. 4 (Spring 1964), pp. 327–36.

Gilman, Sander L., 'Black Bodies, White Bodies: Toward an Iconography of Female Sexuality in Late Nineteenth-century Art, Medicine and Literature', *Critical Inquiry* vol. 12 no. 1 (1985), pp. 204–42.

Graham, Allison, *Framing the South: Hollywood, Television, and Race during the Civil Rights Struggle* (Baltimore, MD: Johns Hopkins University Press, 2001).

Harris, Dianne, 'Clean and Bright and Everyone White: Seeing the Postwar Domestic Environment in the United States', in Dianne Harris and D. Fairchild Ruggles (eds), *Sites Unseen: Landscape and Vision* (Pittsburgh, PA: University of Pittsburgh Press, 2007), pp. 241–62.

Haskell, Molly, 'Can TV Actors Make It in the Movies?', *New York Times* (4 February 1979), pp. D1, D32.

Hollinger, Karen, *The Actress: Hollywood Acting and the Female Star* (New York: Routledge, 2006).

hooks, bell, *Black Looks: Race and Representation* (New York: Routledge, 2015).

Langford, Barry, *Post-Classical Hollywood: Film Industry, Style and Ideology since 1945* (Edinburgh: Edinburgh University Press, 2010).

Lasch, Christopher, *Haven in a Heartless World: The Family Besieged* (New York: Basic Books, 1977).

Lawford, Peter, Natalie Wood Interview (1975). Accessed 25 November 2011 from http://www.youtube.com/watch?y=u8c ZgqqNrG4.

Lawrence, Amy. 'Losing Her Voice: Silencing Two Daughters of Hollywood', *Style* vol. 35 no. 2 (2001), pp. 219–36.

Leibman, Nina C., 'Sexual Misdemeanor/Psychoanalytic Felony', *Cinema Journal* vol. 26 no. 2 (Winter 1987), pp. 27–38.

Leibman, Nina C., 'The Way We Weren't: Abortion 1950s Style in *Blue Denim* and *Our Time*', *Velvet Light Trap* vol. 29 (Spring 1992), pp. 31–42.

Leibman, Nina C., *Living Room Lectures: The Fifties Family in Film and Television* (Austin: University of Texas Press, 1995).

Levy, Emmanuel, 'Inside Daisy Clover', *Emanuellevy Cinema 24/7* (23 March 2009). Accessed 5 May 2015 from http://emanuellevy. com/review/inside-daisy-clover-1965-1/.

Loizidou, Elena, 'Rebellion and Citizenship: Hannah Arendt, Jim Stark, and American Public Life in the 1950s', in J. David Slocum (ed.), *Rebel Without a Cause: Approaches to a Maverick Masterwork* (Albany: SUNY Press, 2005), pp. 191–208.

Loveman, Mara and Jeronimo O. Muniz, 'How Puerto Rico Became White: Boundary Dynamics and Intercensus Racial Reclassification', *American Sociological Review* vol. 72 (December 2007), pp. 915–39.

Lucia, Cynthia, 'Natalie Wood: Studio Stardom and Hollywood in Transition', in Cynthia Lucia, Roy Grundmann and Art Simon (eds), *The Wiley-Blackwell History of American Film, Volume III 1946 to 1975* (Malden, MA: Wiley-Blackwell, 2012), pp. 26–61.

Lury, Karen, *The Child in Film: Tears, Fears and Fairytales* (London: I. B. Tauris, 2010).

Mailer, Norman, *Advertisements for Myself* (New York: G. P. Putnam and Sons, 1959).

Mazursky, Paul, *Show Me the Magic* (New York: Simon & Schuster, 1999).

McLeland, Susan, 'Elizabeth Taylor: Hollywood's Last Glamour Girl', in Hilary Radner and Moya Luckett (eds), *Swinging Single: Representing Sexuality in the 1960s* (Minneapolis: University of Minnesota Press, 1999), pp. 227–53.

McNally, Karen, *When Frankie Went to Hollywood: Frank Sinatra and American Male Identity* (Urbana: University of Illinois Press, 2008).

Medovoi, Leerom, *Rebels: Youth and the Cold War Origins of Identity* (Durham, NC: Duke University Press, 2005).

Mills, Brett, *Television Sitcom* (London: BFI, 2005).

Moore, Dick, *Twinkle Twinkle Little Star. But Don't Have Sex or Take the Car* (New York: Harper & Row, 1984a).

Moran, Jeffrey P., *Teaching Sex: The Shaping of Adolescence in the 20th Century* (Cambridge, MA: Harvard University Press, 2000).

Mordden, Ethan, *Medium Cool: The Movies of the 1960s* (New York: Alfred A. Knopf, 1990).

Naremore, James, *Acting in the Cinema* (Berkeley: University of California Press, 1988).

Negra, Diane, *Off-White Hollywood: American Culture and Ethnic Female Stardom* (New York: Routledge, 2001).

Negrón-Muntaner, Frances, 'Feeling Pretty: *West Side Story* and Puerto Rican Identity Discourses', *Social Text* vol. 18 no. 2 (Summer 2000), pp. 83–106.

O'Connor, Jane, *The Cultural Significance of the Child Star* (New York: Routledge, 2008).

Ogilvie, Jessica P., 'How Hollywood Keeps Out Women', *L.A. Weekly* (29 April 2015). Accessed 3 May 2015 from http://www.laweekly.com/news/how-hollywood-keeps-out-women-5525034.

Packard, Vance, *The Sexual Wilderness: The Contemporary Upheaval in Male–Female Relationships* (New York: Pocket Books, 1970).

Parsons, Talcott, 'Youth in the Context of American Society', in Erik H. Erikson (ed.), *Youth: Change and Challenge* (New York: Anchor Books, 1963), pp. 110–42.

Pells, Richard, 'The Peculiar Generation', *Chronicle of Higher Education* (21 March 2010). Accessed 30 May 2015 from http://chronicle.com/article/The-Peculiar-Generation/64695/.

Pullen, Kirsten, *Like a Natural Woman: Spectacular Female Performance in Classical Hollywood* (New Brunswick, NJ: Rutgers University Press, 2014).

Ray, Nicholas, *I Was Interrupted: Nicholas Ray on Making Movie*s (Berkeley: University of California Press, 1993).

Rowe, Aimee Carrillo and Samantha Lindsey, 'Reckoning Loyalties: White Femininity as "Crisis"', *Feminist Media Studies* vol. 3 no. 2 (2003), pp. 173–91.

Sammond, Nicholas, *Babes in Tomorrowland: Walt Disney and the Making of the American Child 1936–1960* (Durham, NC: Duke University Press, 2005).

Savran, David, *Taking It Like a Man: White Masculinity, Masochism and Contemporary American Culture* (Princeton, NJ: Princeton University Press, 1998).

Scheiner, Georganne, *Signifying Female Adolescence: Film Representations and Fans, 1920–1950* (Westport, CT: Praeger, 2000).

Smith, Stacy L. and Crystal Allene Cook, 'Gender Stereotypes: An Analysis of Popular Films and TV', Geena Davis Institute, 2008.

Smith, Susan, *Elizabeth Taylor* (London: BFI, 2012).

Sullivan, Rebecca, 'Postwar Virginity and the Marjorie Phenomenon', in Tamar Jeffers McDonald (ed.), *Virgin Territory: Representing Sexual Inexperience in Film* (Detroit, MI: Wayne State University Press, 2010), pp. 68–82.

Wexman, Virginia Wright, *Creating the Couple: Love, Marriage, and Hollywood Performance* (Princeton, NJ: Princeton University Press, 1993).

Wojcik, Pamela Robertson, 'Typecasting', *Criticism* vol. 45 no. 2 (Spring 2003), pp. 223–49.

Wolfe, Tom, *The Pump House Gang* (New York: Farrar, Straus & Giroux, 1968).

Wolfe, Tom, 'The Me Decade and the Third Great Awakening', *New York Magazine* (23 August 1976).

Young, Jeff, *Kazan: The Master Director Discusses His Films* (New York: Newmarket Press, 1999).

Biographies

Finstad, Suzanne, *Natasha: The Biography of Natalie Wood* (New York: Three Rivers Press, 2001).

Lambert, Gavin, *Natalie Wood: A Life* (New York: Alfred A. Knopf, 2004).

Wagner, Robert, *Pieces of My Heart: A Life* (New York: Harper Luxe, 2008).

Wood, Lana, *Natalie: A Memoir by Her Sister* (New York: Dell Publishing Co., Inc., 1984).

Popular Magazine and Archival Sources

All the Fine Young Cannibals plot synopsis, PCA Files. Margaret Herrick Library (22 May 1959).

'At Home with Natalie Wood and Robert Wagner', *Good Housekeeping* (June 1976), pp. 134–9.

Bart, Peter, 'Natalie in Analysis', *New York Times* (3 July 1966), p. 45.

Bascombe, Laura, 'Natalie on the Rebound', *Photoplay* (November 1963), pp. 42–3, 92–4.

'Beauty and Violence', *Look* (11 April 1961), pp. 105–9.

Benner, Ralph, 'The Day I Met Natalie', *Hollywood Studio Magazine* (1988), pp. 30–1.

Berges, Marshall, 'Natalie Wood and Robert Wagner', *Los Angeles Times Home Magazine* (9 October 1979), pp. 42–5.

Block, Maxine, 'How Far Should a Parent Go?', *Photoplay* (March 1956), pp. 72–3, 111–13.

'Bob & Natalie's Wedding', *Photoplay* (October 1972), pp. 34–6, 102–7.

'Born to Be a Star: Photographed for LIFE by Bill Ray', *Life* (20 December 1963), pp. 182–6.

'Boy-crazy Teen-ager', *Movieland* (March 1956), pp. 34–7, 80–1.

Clein, Harry, 'Natalie Wood: On Acting, Nudity, and Growing Up in Hollywood', *Entertainment World* (30 January 1970), pp. 7–9.

Connolly, Mike, 'Rambling Reporter', *Hollywood Reporter* (28 January 1959), p. 2.

Crowley, Walter, 'Natalie Says Yes to Warren … but Warren Says No to Marriage', *Photoplay* (June 1962), pp. 20–1, 93–5.

Crowther, Bosley, 'Where Are the Women?', *New York Times* (23 January 1966), p. 93.

Cuskelly, Richard, 'In 1974 It Is Mrs. Wagner not Ms Wood', *Los Angeles Herald Examiner* (13 October 1974), pp. E1–2.

'Date Bait', *Photoplay* (May 1956), p. 55.

Davidson, Bill, 'Hollywood Throwback', *Saturday Evening Post* (7 April 1962), pp. 32–6.

Dektar, Joan A., 'A Mix of Our Own …', *House Beautiful* (June 1976), pp. 51–7.

Gehman, Richard, 'Don't Sell Natalie Short, part I,' *Photoplay* (August 1957a), pp. 52–3, 90–2.

Gehman, Richard, 'Don't Sell Natalie Short, part II', *Photoplay* (September 1957b), pp. 60–1, 92–4.

Geoffrey Shurlock to Warner Bros, *Rebel Without a Cause* PCA Files. Margaret Herrick Library (31 March 1955).

Greenfeld, Josh, 'Paul Mazursky in Wonderland', *Life* (4 September 1970), pp. 51–7.

Hallowell, John, 'Glamor Gets the Gate as the "Uglies" Come into Their Own', *Life* (24 May 1968), pp. 109–10.

Hallowell, John, 'I'm Going to Live My Life', *New York Times* (9 March 1969), p. D13.

Hoffman, Jim, 'Here Comes the Bride', *Photoplay* (February 1962), pp. 58–61, 85–8.

'Hollywood and the Stars: Natalie Wood', Metro-Goldwyn-Mayer (*circa* March–April 1964). Accessed 25 November 2011 from http://www.youtube.com/watch?v=QkCIsH0OzKo.

Hopper, Hedda, 'Child Star to Glamor Girl', *Chicago Tribune Magazine* (26 June 1955), p. 22.

'How Bob Changed Natalie/How Natalie Changed Bob', *Movieland* (April 1958), pp. 42–3, 69–71.

Hull, Bob, 'About Natalie Wood and "The Big Party"', *Los Angeles Herald & Express* (8 October 1959), p. B6.

Hyams, Joe, 'Natalie Wood Heard From', *New York Tribune* (20 June 1957), n.p.

Inside Daisy Clover, PCA Analysis of Film Content, Margaret Herrick Library (9 November 1965).

Kareda, Urjo, 'The Signals Movie Actors Give', *New York Times* (11 August 1974), pp. 97, 11.

Kashner, Sam, 'Natalie Wood's Fatal Voyage', *Vanity Fair* (March 2000), pp. 214–33.

Klemesrud, Judy, 'Natalie Wood's Real-Life Romantic Comedy', *New York Times* (10 February 1980), p. 58.

Korba, Anthony, 'Natalie: More than the Hollywood Stereotype', *Orange Coast Magazine* (October 1979), pp. 11–17.

Land, Jon, 'Happily Ever After', *Saturday Evening Post* (March 1979), pp. 83–5, 108.

Lane, Laura, 'Natalie Wood's Diary: A Lady on the Loose', *Photoplay* (December 1956), pp. 48–9, 97–8.

Lardine, Bob, 'A Star Is Born Again', *New York Daily News Sunday Magazine* (11 February 1979), pp. 22–6, 36.

'The Last Studio Star', *E! True Hollywood Story*, Season 1, Episode 22 (1997).

Lawrence, James, 'Natalie Wood and Bob Wagner in Love Again', *Photoplay* (June 1972), pp. 38–9, 111.

Lewis, Joseph, 'Whatever Happened to Baby Natalie?', *Cosmopolitan* (November 1968), pp. 132–6, 177.

Loewell, Alis, 'The Natalie Wood Interview', *Los Angeles Free Press* (2 August 1974), pp. 22–5.

Lyle, Jae, 'This Is the Story of Beautiful Women and the Hollywood Tragedy That Haunts Them', *Photoplay* (November 1961).

Mann, May, 'Bob and Natalie Talk about Their Marriage', *Movieland and TV Time* (August 1960), pp. 44–5, 56–7.

Maynard, John, 'Young Veteran in Starry Quest', *New York Times* (19 April 1964), p. X7.

McDonald, Thomas, 'Presenting a Happy "Act": Wagner and Wood', *New York Times* (14 June 1959), p. X7.

Meltsir, Aljean, 'Too Old to Spank', *Motion Picture Magazine* (May 1956), pp. 21, 58–7.

Meltsir, Aljean, 'The Taming of the Shrewd', *Coronet* (February 1960), pp. 127–34.

'Miss Wood Wins Praise of Director', USC Warner Bros. Archives 1956 [no identifying information].

Moore, Dick, 'At Last a Visit with Natalie Wood', *McCall's* (October 1984b), pp. 52–6, 167.

'Movie Star into Actress: The Story of Natalie Wood', *Newsweek* (26 February 1962), pp. 54–7.

'Natalie Waves Thanks for Nothing', *Life* (6 May 1966), p. 44.

Natalie Wood Interview with Peter Lawford (1975). Accessed 25 November 2011 from http://www.youtube.com/watch?v= u8cZgqqNrG4.

'Natalie Wood on Marriage to Robert Wagner', USC Warner Bros. Archives (18 April 1959).

'Natalie Wood: Our Sexual Conscience on the Silver Screen?', *L'Officiel/USA* (August 1980), pp. 118–19.

'New Movie Moppet', *Life* (26 November 1945), pp. 87–8.

Nicholas Ray description of Judy, USC Warner Bros. Archives (13 December 1954).

Nicholas Ray memo to Jack Warner, USC Warner Bros. Archives (1 March 1955).

Oakes, Philip, 'Natalie Wood: Still Shining Bright', *London Sunday Times* (28 December 1969).

Ott, Beverly, 'Junior Femme Fatale', *Photoplay* (June 1956), pp. 35–7, 102–6.

Parsons, Louella, 'Endsville', *Modern Screen* (June 1960), pp. 28–31, 58–9.

Pecheco, Patrick, 'And in This Corner … Natalie Wood, Back for Another Round', *After Dark* (October 1979), pp. 34–9.

Phelps, Robert, 'Self-Education of a Brilliant Highbrow', *Life* (21 January 1966), p. 8.

Pope, Elizabeth, 'What Hollywood Does to Women', *Good Housekeeping* (June 1962), pp. 32–7.

Reed, Rex, 'Shirley, Far from the Hollywood Crowd', *New York Times* (26 February 1967), p. D13.

Reynolds, Patricia, 'Natalie Wood's Own Story', *Pageant* (July 1971), pp. 46–57.

Robinson, Michael and Frederic Christian, 'For Fun, I Work', *Cosmopolitan* (June 1957), pp. 45–52.

See, Carolyn, 'The Recycling of Natalie Wood', *McCall's* (August 1979), pp. 16–18, 24–5, 131.

Sheppard, Gene, 'Natalie Wood: She Wanted Yesterday ...', *Hollywood Studio Magazine* (1988), pp. 6–11.

Splendor in the Grass pressbook. USC Warner Bros. Archives (August 1961).

'The Strange Doings of an Actress at Practice', *Life* (28 January 1957), pp. 97–100.

'Teenage Tiger', *Look* (25 June 1957), pp. 95–7.

Thompson, Douglas, 'Natalie Wood's Kiss of Life', *London Daily Mail* (7 April 1979), p. 21.

Thompson, Thomas, 'Natalie Wood and Robert Wagner Get It Together Again', *Cosmopolitan* (August 1975).

Thompson, Thomas, 'Natalie Wood: Hollywood's Number One Survivor', *Look* (April 1979), pp. 5–16.

Tibbetts, John, 'Natalie Wood: A Life on Film', *American Classic Screen* (March/April 1982), pp. 20–2, 30.

'Turner Classic Movies Tribute: Natalie Wood'. Accessed 29 May 2015 from https://www.youtube.com/watch?v=x7mehiZCpD0

Tusher, Bill, 'Going Steady with Stardom', *Motion Picture Magazine* (1956[?]), pp. 55, 64–5.

Waterbury, Ruth, 'The Strange Story of Two Beautiful Sisters Who Love and Lose ... and Lose ... and Lose!', *Photoplay* (August 1966), pp. 28–9, 76–8.

Whitman, Arthur, 'Why Must Everything I Do Bring on Lectures on Morality?', *Pageant* (June 1967), pp. 31–7.

Wilcock, John, 'She Took on Hollywood ... and Won', *Star Weekly Magazine* (4 July 1959), pp. 16–17, 28.

Wilson, Liza, 'Hollywood's "teeniest' star"', *Washington Post and Times Herald* (19 August 1956), p. AW20.

Wood, Natalie, 'You Haven't Heard the Half about Jimmy', *Photoplay* (November 1955), pp. 55, 82–4.

Zimmerann, Gereon, 'Natalie Wood: Child of Change', *Look* (13 August 1963), pp. 90–5.

Movie Reviews

Adler, Renata, 'The Current Cinema', *New Yorker* (27 August 1966), pp. 88–9.

Alpert, Hollis, 'Instant Tennessee Williams', *Saturday Review* no. 49 (25 June 1966), p. 40.

'Boardinghouse Reach', *Newsweek* (1 August 1966), pp. 83–4.

Canby, Vincent, 'Bob & Carol & Ted & Alice Twits "New Morality"', *New York Times* (17 September 1969), p. 50.

Canby, Vincent, 'Reassurances of "Last Married Couple"', *New York Times* (8 February 1980), p. C12.

Crowther, Bosley, 'Musical Advance: The "West Side Story" Expands on Screen', *New York Times* (22 October 1961), p. X1.

Crowther, Bosley, 'Natalie Wood Cast as Camille in Dixieland', *New York Times* (4 August 1966), p. 24.

Cuskelly, Richard, 'In 1974 It Is Mrs. Wagner Not Ms Wood', *Los Angeles Herald Examiner* (13 October 1974), pp. E1-2.

Cuskelly, Richard, 'Michael Caine Is a Peeper', *Los Angeles Herald Examiner* (December 1975).

Ebert, Roger, 'Bob & Carol & Ted & Alice', originally published in *Chicago Sun Times* (22 December 1969). Accessed 30 May 2015 from http://www.rogerebert.com/reviews/bob-and-carol-and-ted-and-alice-1969.

Johnson, Albert, 'Beige, Brown or Black', *Film Quarterly* vol. 13 no. 1 (Autumn 1959), p. 41.

Kael, Pauline, '"The Innocents", and What Passes for Experience', *Film Quarterly* vol. 15 no. 4 (Summer 1962), pp. 21–36.

Kael, Pauline, 'Waiting for Orgy,' *New Yorker* (4 October 1969), pp. 144, 147–9.

'Kings Go Forth', *Newsweek* (30 June 1958), p. 82.

Knight, Arthur, 'Romeo Revisted [sic]', *Saturday Review* no. 14 (October 1961), p. 40.

Maslin, Janet, 'Film: More for the Grown-ups', *New York Times* (26 August 1979), p. 59.

O'Connor, John J., 'This Tribute Smacks of Exploitation', *New York Times* (5 December 1976), p. 133.

Schlesinger, Arthur, 'Expert Satire', *Vogue* (1 November 1969), p. 118.

'Sweetness & Blight', *Time* (20 October 1961), p. 94.

'Tragedy in Overdrive', *Newsweek* (October 1961), pp. 101–2.

FILMOGRAPHY

Feature Films

HAPPY LAND (Irving Pichel, USA, 1943), Little Girl Who Drops
   Ice Cream Cone (uncredited)
TOMORROW IS FOREVER (Irving Pichel, USA, 1946), Margaret
   Ludwig
THE BRIDE WORE BOOTS (Irving Pichel, USA, 1946), Carol
   Warren
THE GHOST AND MRS. MUIR (Joseph L. Mankiewicz, USA,
   1947), Anna Muir as a Child
MIRACLE ON 34TH STREET (George Seaton, USA, 1947),
   Susan Walker
DRIFTWOOD (Allan Dwan, USA, 1947), Jenny Hollingsworth
SCUDDA HOO! SCUDDA HAY! (F. Hugh Herbert, USA, 1948),
   Eufraznee 'Bean' McGill
CHICKEN EVERY SUNDAY (George Seaton, USA, 1949), Ruth
   Hefferan
THE GREEN PROMISE (William D. Russell, USA, 1949), Susan
   Matthews
FATHER WAS A FULLBACK (John M. Stahl, USA, 1949), Ellen
   Cooper
NO SAD SONGS FOR ME (Rudolph Maté, USA, 1950), Polly
   Scott

OUR VERY OWN (David Miller, USA, 1950), Penny Macaulay

NEVER A DULL MOMENT (George Marshall, USA, 1950), Nan

THE JACKPOT (Walter Lang, USA, 1950), Phyllis Lawrence

DEAR BRAT (William A. Seiter, USA, 1951), Pauline

THE BLUE VEIL (Curtis Bernhardt, USA, 1951), Stephanie
Rawlins

THE ROSE BOWL STORY (William Beaudine, USA, 1952), Sally
Burke

JUST FOR YOU (Elliott Nugent, USA, 1952), Barbara Blake

THE STAR (Stuart Heisler, USA, 1952), Gretchen

THE SILVER CHALICE (Victor Saville, USA, 1954), Helena as a
Girl

ONE DESIRE (Jerry Hopper, USA, 1955), Seely Dowder

REBEL WITHOUT A CAUSE (Nicholas Ray, USA, 1955), Judy

THE SEARCHERS (John Ford, USA, 1956), Debbie Edwards –
Age 15

A CRY IN THE NIGHT (Frank Tuttle, USA, 1956), Elizabeth

THE BURNING HILLS (Stuart Heisler, USA, 1956), Maria-
Christina Colton

THE GIRL HE LEFT BEHIND (David Butler, USA, 1956), Susan
Daniels

BOMBERS B-52 (Gordon Douglas, USA, 1957), Lois Brennan

MARJORIE MORNINGSTAR (Irving Rapper, USA, 1958),
Marjorie Morgenstern

KINGS GO FORTH (Delmer Daves, USA, 1958), Monique Blair

CASH MCCALL (Joseph Pevney, USA, 1960), Lory Austen

ALL THE FINE YOUNG CANNIBALS (Michael Anderson, USA,
1960), Sarah 'Salome' Davis

SPLENDOR IN THE GRASS (Elia Kazan, USA, 1961), Wilma
Dean Loomis

WEST SIDE STORY (Robert Wise, USA, 1961), Maria

GYPSY (Mervyn LeRoy, USA, 1962), Louise Hovick/Gypsy Rose
Lee

LOVE WITH THE PROPER STRANGER (Robert Mulligan, USA, 1963), Angie Rossini

SEX AND THE SINGLE GIRL (Richard Quine, USA, 1964), Helen Brown

THE GREAT RACE (Blake Edwards, USA, 1965), Maggie Dubois

INSIDE DAISY CLOVER (Robert Mulligan, USA, 1965) Daisy Clover

THIS PROPERTY IS CONDEMNED (Sydney Pollack, USA, 1966), Alva Starr

PENELOPE (Arthur Hiller, USA, 1966), Penelope

BOB & CAROL & TED & ALICE (Paul Mazursky, USA, 1969), Carol Sanders

DOWNHILL RACER (Michael Ritchie, USA, 1969), Uncredited

THE CANDIDATE (Michael Ritchie, USA, 1972), Natalie Wood

PEEPER (Peter Hyams, USA, 1976), Ellen Prendergast

METEOR (Ronald Neame, USA, 1979), Tatiana Donskaya

THE LAST MARRIED COUPLE IN AMERICA (Gilbert Cates, USA, 1980), Mari Thompson

BRAINSTORM (Douglas Trumbull, USA, 1983), Karen Brace

Teleplays, Television Movies and Television Miniseries

THE PEPSI-COLA PLAYHOUSE: PLAYMATES (Richard Irving, USA, 1954), Monica

GENERAL ELECTRIC THEATER: I'M A FOOL (Don Medford, USA, 1954), Lucy

GENERAL ELECTRIC THEATER: FEATHERTOP (USA, 1955), Polly Gookin

MAX LIEBMAN SPECTACULARS: HEIDI (Max Liebman, USA, 1955), Klara Sesseman

STUDIO ONE IN HOLLYWOOD: MIRACLE AT POTTER'S
FARM (Franklin J. Schaffner, USA, 1955), Jen Potter
FOUR STAR PLAYHOUSE: THE WILD BUNCH (USA, 1955),
Louise
THE FORD TELEVISION THEATRE: TOO OLD FOR DOLLS
(Fred. F. Sears, USA, 1955), Polly Ramsay
WARNER BROTHERS PRESENTS: THE DEADLY RIDDLE
(Don Weis, USA, 1956), ?
THE KAISER ALUMINUM HOUR: CARNIVAL (George Roy
Hill, USA, 1956), Kathy Jo
THE AFFAIR (Gilbert Cates, USA, 1973), Courtney Patterson
CAT ON A HOT TIN ROOF (Robert Moore, USA, 1976), Maggie
'The Cat'
FROM HERE TO ETERNITY (Buzz Kulik, USA, 1979), Karen
Holmes
THE CRACKER FACTORY (TV Movie) (Burt Brinckerhoff,
USA, 1979), Cassie Barrett
THE MEMORY OF EVA RYKER (TV Movie) (Walter Grauman,
USA, 1980), Eva Ryker / Claire Ryker

Television Continuing Series (including Guest Stars)

MAYOR OF THE TOWN (USA, 1954), June/Mayor's Niece
THE PRIDE OF THE FAMILY (USA, 1953–4), Ann Morrison
KINGS ROW (USA, 1955–6), Renee Gyllinson
CONFLICT (USA, 1957), Girl on the Subway
SWITCH (USA, 1975), Uncredited
SWITCH (USA, 1978), Girl in the Bubble Bath
HART TO HART (USA, 1979), Natasha Gurdin

INDEX

Page numbers in **bold** indicate detailed analysis; those in *italic* denote illustrations.

List of Illustrations

While considerable effort has been made to correctly identify the copyright
holders, this has not been possible in all cases. We apologise for any apparent
negligence and any omissions or corrections brought to our attention will be
remedied in any future editions.

Inside Daisy Clover, Park Place Productions/Warner Bros.; *Splendor in the Grass*,
NBI Company/Newtown Productions; *Tomorrow Is Forever*, International
Pictures/RKO Radio Pictures; *Miracle on 34th Street*, Twentieth Century-Fox
Film Corporation; *The Green Promise*, RKO Radio Pictures/Glenn McCarthy
Production; *The Searchers*, C.V. Whitney Pictures Company/Warner Bros.;
Rebel Without a Cause, © Warner Bros. Pictures Inc.; *This Property Is Condemned*,
© Seven Arts Productions; *All the Fine Young Cannibals*, Avon Productions/Loew's
Incorporated; *Kings Go Forth*, Frank Ross Productions/Eton Productions; *West
Side Story*, © Beta Productions; *Bob & Carol & Ted & Alice*, Columbia Pictures
Industries Inc.; *Cat on a Hot Tin Roof*, Granada Television; *The Last Married
Couple in America*, Cates Brothers Company/Universal Pictures; *Brainstorm*,
© MGM/UA Entertainment.